KARATE

KARATE

DAVID MITCHELL

Crescent Books

Produced by
Brompton Books Corporation
15 Sherwood Place,
Greenwich
Connecticut CT 06830.

This 1990 edition published by
CRESCENT,
distributed by Outlet Book Company, Inc.,
a Random House Company,
225 Park Avenue South,
New York, New York 10003.

Printed and bound in Hong Kong.

ISBN 0-517-05190-7

10 9 8 7 6 5 4 3 2 1

Photo credits

The author and publishers would like to thank Martin Sellars who
took the majority of the pictures used in this book. Thanks also to the
following for the pictures on the pages noted.
Mark Bishop: page 13 (left).
Sylvio Dokov: pages 9 (both), 11 (right), 13 (right), 14, 15 (left).
Peter Lewis: page 13 (left).

Dedication

I would like to dedicate this book to my bank manager,
Ian Taylor, whose kind forbearance has made it possible
for me to eat during its writing.

Page 1: Wado ryu basic punching practise operates from a low
straddle stance.
Page 2: Wado ryu stylists demonstrate a planned sparring sequence.
Page 3: A graphic demonstration of the athletic skills required of a high
grade karateka.
Page 4, left: Shotokan back stance is very long and the hips
face forward.
Page 4, right: The Shito ryu version of lunge punch begins from a free
sparring stance.
Page 5, left: Kyokushinkai front kick; note how the supporting foot has
swivelled outward as the kicking leg has advanced.
Page 5, right: A Shito ryu stylist demonstrates a knife block.

CONTENTS

Foreword   7

Introduction   8

The History and Philosophy of Karate   10
The Development of Karate Styles   11
The Nature of Karate   14

Karate Stances   16
Power Punches   26
Karate Kicks   44
Blocking Techniques   56
Sparring   70
Training Methods   74

FOREWORD

Different karate styles have their own terminology and this precludes me from using Japanese expressions. Sometimes different names are given to the same technique. Thus one style uses the name 'inner forearm block block' to describe what another calls 'outer forearm block'. I have therefore tried to use common terms wherever possible, though the odd technical term nevertheless crops up from time to time.

There are many fascinating similarities (and differences) between the kata of each style. However, to describe such would take us well beyond the scope of this book. As it is, I have compared the basic techniques of each style and will leave the kata to another day.

Finally, although this book sets out to compare the styles of karate, it in no way attempts to do so in a way that implies that one is better than another. As any senior coach will tell you, there is no best style; it is the person inside the karate tunic that makes the style – not the other way round.

David Mitchell,
March 1990

Important advice for readers

The practice of any martial art whether individually or with an opponent may be hazardous. Readers are advised that under no circumstances should they practice any of the techniques demonstrated in this book without proper supervision, safety precautions and tuition. Despite the best precautions accidents can and do happen. Risks should be minimised by training with a coach approved and registered with an appropriate official body.

All of the chief instructors featured in this book are members of Britain's **Martial Arts Commission**. This body is the only such organisation which is recognised by the government-sponsored Sports Council. The Martial Arts Commission has a scheme to register approved instructors. In the United States **US Karate Inc.** is the only governing body recognised by the World Union of Karatedo Organisations (WUKO). WUKO represents karate on the International Olympic Committee.

Addresses of recognised instructors can therefore be obtained from:

US Karate Inc,
1326 Orlando Avenue
PO Box 8223
Akron
Ohio 44320

The Martial Arts Commission
First Floor
Broadway House
15-16 Deptford Broadway
London SE8 4PE

Acknowledgments

The author and publishers have great pleasure in acknowledging the considerable help and expertise provided by the following leading exponents of British Karate.

George Andrews is Chief Instructor to the British division of the International Goju Ryu Federation. George is a 5th dan and has been training for 22 years. He has his own dojo in southeast London.

Frank Perry is a 6th dan kyoshi grade Chief Instructor in Seiki Jukyu Karate. Previously Frank trained in Kyokushinkai karate, though he does not do so now. Frank has his own dojo in southwest London.

Tommy Morris is a 6th dan in Tani ha Shito ryu and the World Chief Referee for WUKO and the European Union. He is official coach to the Egyptian Karate Federation and has his own dojo in Glasgow.

Paul Perry is a 5th dan in Shotokan, having trained under the illustrious Kanazawa Hirokazu. He has his own association – the Jin Sei Kai – and trains in the north London area.

Peter Spanton is a 6th dan of the Wado ryu style. He has been training for more than 24 years and is chief instructor to the Higashi Karate Kai. Peter has his own dojo in east London.

The author and publishers would also like to thank Linda Marchant (1st dan), Carl David (3rd dan), Sue Spillard (1st dan), Stephen Morris (3rd dan), John Howard (3rd dan), Anneli Densham (2nd dan), John Kerridge (1st dan) and Sue Skinner (3rd dan) for their willing help and considerable expertise.

Finally, a second thank you to Frank Perry for allowing us to film in his excellent Twickenham dojo.

Front row, left to right: George Andrews, Frank Perry, Tommy Morris. *Back row:* Paul Perry and Peter Spanton.

INTRODUCTION

This book is about the various styles of karate practised in the present day. It is not a comparison from the point of view of showing which is the more refined system – for as we shall shortly see, that is largely irrelevant. It simply looks at some fairly basic techniques and sees how they are practised in these different styles. Before launching into a description of those techniques, it will be as well to agree on what karate is (and isn't!).

What follows may appear controversial but it is nevertheless a valid view. The object will be to get you, the reader, to consider what exactly karate is.

In the strict sense of the word, karate is not a 'martial' art. You can check this statement out for yourselves if you happen to have a dictionary on hand. My dictionary defines martial as 'relating to or characteristic of war, soldiers, or the military life'. Art is defined variously as 'method, facility or knack; a system of rules governing a particular human activity.'

To the best of my knowledge, karate has never formed part, as such, of a military training program. This is not to say that individual soldiers may not have studied karate; neither is it to claim that karate training has never been used to increase aggression in civilians who might one day become potential conscripts. The plain fact is that karate has never formed part of any formal military training manual, unlike the Korean martial art of tae-kwondo. If we therefore accept the precise meaning of the words, karate is not a martial art at all, though we may refer to it as a fighting art.

The second myth surrounding karate is the notion that there is a part of it which can be described as 'traditional'. Once again I turn to my trusty dictionary and note that tradition is 'a specific custom or practice of long standing'. Can an activity which is effectively less than 100 years old have any part which is traditional?

No less a personage than Fusajiro Takagi, a 9th dan practising karateka and the previous chairman of the ruling Japan Karate Federation agrees with this view and criticises those who claim to practise 'traditional' karate as people without knowledge. As he rightly says, these 'traditional karateka' must be studying kung fu!

The third myth is that Karate is an effective system of self defense. This may (and I use the word 'may' advisedly) be the case in the same way that a gun is an effective way of killing someone. It takes a person to use the gun correctly in order for it to be effective. Karate may well confer the potential for being effective upon a student though it is worth pointing out that a coward who learns karate eventually becomes a cowardly black belt! Many people seem to think that the studying of karate will make them brave, courageous and capable. It will not. The potential offered by any fighting system ultimately depends upon the person learning it. Even the most ineffectual system can be dangerous when in the hands of a psychopath!

I do not see how karate can be advertised as a means of self defense when 99.99 percent of those who teach it as such have no practical knowledge of what constitutes self defense. It used to be that the effectiveness of a martial art was tested on the battlefield and ineffectual techniques tended to eliminate the user. Though very simplistic, I nevertheless believe that this 'military darwinism' also holds good in self defense terms. But how is self defense to be tested? Which karate instructors regularly use self defense? The emphasis here is on use of the word 'regular'.

Furthermore, is the 250-pound fourth dan black belt justified in saying that because a technique once worked for him, it will also work for a 100-pound novice on a twelve week self defense course?

The fourth myth is that karate techniques are necessarily powerful. They probably are powerful in the hands of a powerful person and in some cases, I would say that a person could deliver a powerful blow *in spite of* inherent shortcomings found in many techniques. This myth of karate power has come about because some techniques pit agonist muscle against antagonist muscle and thereby feel powerful.

Yet I have seen these same 'killing blows' strike with full force upon the solar plexus of an opponent and have absolutely no effect! I always remember World Chief Referee Tommy Morris's acute observation gained from decades of elite refereeing experience. He observed that people were most often knocked out or bowled over by wild blows which totally lacked any karate focussing technique.

The Japanese habit is to train people in class lines, such that they practise techniques 'unloaded' – i.e., without resistance. But if you perform a roundhouse kick against no resistance, the technique must be modified to prevent you from falling over. You therefore learn a modified technique which, when applied for the first time against a resistance, causes you to strike without power and/or fall over!

There is no doubt that karate blows can become fairly powerful once training is adapted. However, as I shall indicate in the subsequent chapter on karate's history, the art's potential effectiveness has suffered greatly from the teaching methods imposed upon it by the early Japanese teachers.

The fifth myth about karate is that practising it makes you fit. I would not object quite so strongly if the words '. . . for practising karate' were added to the previous sentence. It is a known fact that the body adapts accurately to the loading placed upon it. Therefore if you regularly train hard in karate, you will become fit to train hard in karate! In other words, any fitness benefit accrued is highly specific.

There is a growing body of medical evidence to suggest that far from making you fit, the way karate is practised by a great many of its exponents can actually cause injuries! Unloaded techniques performed over a period of time appear to cause permanent joint injury; the elbow, knee and sacro-iliac joints are very much at risk. People sometimes dispute this but I invite them to consider the general health of top practitioners and come to their own conclusions.

Two terms are much bandied about in karate and Japanese martial art circles. *Jutsu* basically means 'art' and *Do* means 'Way'. Traditional martial arts relied equally upon mental and physical aspects. The physical aspect was the tradition of proven technique and the mental aspect, the philosophy needed to control the use of those techniques. Each was useless without the other; for what is the good of a highly skilled warrior who runs away from the enemy, or a resolute warrior without weapons skill? The frightened or angry warrior is not likely to fight as effectively as one who is dispassionate.

Karate jutsu attempts to parallel the mental aspect of martial art training by adopting a fairly brutal regime that frightens away all except those of a sado-masochistic disposition. I think this falls far short of the classical methods since they never sought to produce warriors who were simply aggressive or brutal.

The Do is derived from Chinese philosophy and means a way or path to follow. Within karate-do, the reason for practising technique shifts from practical effectiveness to using it as a vehicle to express a philosophy of life. When swords were rendered obsolete by the rifle, fencing continued but for a different reason. The techniques were no longer effective but the philosophy was.

The primary stated objective of karate-do is to conquer the self – not the opponent. This is an end in itself – not as a means towards fighting more efficiently. Consequently, a large number of techniques have become stylised and modified. Karate kata, for example, contain moves which are present for appearance purposes only (I gleefully watch ingenious teachers trying to work out applications for them!) and much of the original purpose of many moves has now been lost.

What, then, is karate? It is the modern-day development of a relatively recent Okinawan fighting system that has undergone major change since its inception. In the hands of a powerful and aggressive individual, it is an effective form of unarmed combat. To the philosopher, it is one of many physical vehicles which can be adapted to minimise the ego. In short, karate is no more and no less than what you, the exponent, put into it.

I hope this introduction has succeeded in stimulating you to rethink your views of karate practice. If nothing else, I hope it has shown you that it is the person not the style or art which is, in the final analysis, most important. Beside this, such things as style differences pale into insignificance. I have never thought that any style of karate confers more benefits than another and it is with this very much in mind that we go on to examine the origins of karate and its present day styles.

Above: WUKO competition is fast, spectacular and involves a low risk of injury because of the high skill level of participants.

Right: WUKO competition brings together all the major styles of karate, unifying them under a common set of rules. The World Cup, held in Budapest, is one of the three major sporting events of the world karate calendar.

The History and Philosophy of Karate

There is no evidence for suggesting that karate or its immediate antecedents existed before the mid-18th century. The greatest known changes in it probably occurred in the early twentieth century and were made in response to a desire to popularise karate among mainland Japanese.

We know that the direct antecedent of karate was the Okinawan fighting system of *to-de,* though this may itself be predated by an earlier form, known simply as *te.*

Okinawa is the largest of the Ryukyu Islands, lying some 450 kilometers to the south west of Japan and 550 kilometers due east of the southern Chinese mainland. Its position therefore put it within the spheres of influence of both those countries. During the early part of the 14th century, the island became divided into three kingdoms – Nanzan in the south, Chuzan in the centre and Hokuzan in the north. The king of Chuzan sought alliance with China and this was granted in 1372. As a consequence of this alliance, a party of 36 Chinese families came to Okinawa in 1393 and settled in the village of Toei. Some of the visitors were martial artists.

In 1429 the three kingdoms were unified by King Sho Hashi. His successor, Sho Shin, subsequently imposed a ban both on the wearing of swords and on the ownership of private armories. Okinawa was annexed by Japan in February 1609, following invasion by a force of 3000 warriors of the warlike Satsuma clan but initially, there was little interference in the island's domestic affairs.

In 1661 the Chinese sent Kong Shang Kung, a military attaché, to Okinawa. He taught Chinese martial art to two Okinawans, Sakugawa Satunushi and Yari Kitan. Sakugawa was already a famous exponent of Okinawan martial art and he may well have combined the two systems together to form the basis of what came to be known as *shuri-te* ('Hand of Shuri'). Kong Shang Kung was not the only visiting teacher and other notables were known by their Okinawan names of Chinto, Waishinzan, Iwah and Ason. However, the continuing ban on martial art weapons meant that only unarmed martial art could be taught.

Okinawans regularly travelled to the Chinese mainland to train under martial art teachers. For example, Yari Chatan, the grandson of Yari Kitan, spent twenty years on the mainland learning Southern Shaolin Kung fu. However, the Japanese overlords eventually became irritated both with Okinawa's continuing alliance with China, and with the presence of Okinawans at the Peking court. This irritation led to restrictions being placed upon permitted travel. The clamp-down caused civil unrest and there were several disturbances, culminating in the destruction of the offices of the Ryukyu Trading Company. This led to even harsher controls. Eventually the island was pacified and became resigned to its new status as a prefecture of Japan.

At least two quite different threads of development took place in the Okinawan fighting arts. On the one hand, a school of covert weaponry arose among the farmers and peasants. Their weapons included the quarterstaff, the sickle, the rice flail, the rice grinder handles and the short trident. Though the major emphasis was laid on weapons practice, unarmed combat was also taught as a secondary system. This system should not be confused with ritual practice – where permitted – using overt martial art weapons by members of the warrior caste. On the other hand, young nobles and members of the merchant class took up the systems taught by the Chinese at Toei, and by mainland teachers.

So far as is known, there is no hard evidence to prove which, if either, of these lines of development led to the relatively widespread practice of to-de in and around the three Okinawan towns of Tomari, Naha and Shuri. Though it is no doubt an over-simplification, the three towns each developed a slightly different expression of to-de. That of the capital, Shuri, became known as *shuri-te.* This was characterised by light, agile movements. As its name implied, *naha-te* is said to have originated in the city of Naha, where it gave rise to forms characterised by strong stances and circular movements. Tomari's styles seemed to combine the features of both shuri- and naha-te. Eventually, as the styles travelled outwards and overlapped, the distinctions between them became somewhat blurred, with naha-te and tomari-te merging to form *shorei ryu* and shuri-te giving rise to *shorin ryu.* Shorin ryu is the Japanese reading of the Chinese characters meaning 'The Shaolin Tradition'.

Toward the end of the nineteenth century, the leading Okinawan masters formed an umbrella liaison and development organisation known as the *Shobukai.* One of its decisions was to rename to-de *karate.* The particular characters used translated as 'China hand', expressing the debt which the Shobukai acknowledged to the Chinese masters. Karate eventually became known to the Japanese and was encouraged as a means of raising the Okinawans' level of aggression. This objective assumed particular importance during 1898 when the overlords imposed military conscription on the islanders.

The chairman of the Shobukai, schoolteacher, Funakoshi Gichin, was responsible for much of the initial promotion of karate. He gave displays for the Japanese navy and in 1917, demonstrated karate before Hirohito, the then crown prince. However, Funakoshi was a poor schoolteacher with an unimpressive ancestry. Moreover he was Okinawan at a time when the islanders were regarded as country bumpkins by the mainland class-ridden Japanese. And to add insult to injury, karate had no tradition worth speaking of! It is therefore hardly surprising that despite those few brief but memorable occasions, karate lapsed into almost total obscurity.

Unable to sustain himself by teaching karate, Funakoshi was obliged to work part-time as a janitor. Indeed, had it not been for his perseverance, karate might well have remained obscure over a far longer period.

Funakoshi met Kano Jigoro, the founder of judo, and noted the way he stressed the scientific application and health-giving training of *jiu jitsu.* So Funakoshi in turn began to stress those same principles in karate and in an effort to make the art more acceptable to the Japanese, he changed its name to 'Way of the Empty Hand'. Though the title remained karate, the Japanese characters were altered to fit the new meaning.

Funakoshi was not the only Okinawan to teach in Japan, but he is probably the single most important, since it is largely through his promotion of a 'Japanified' karate that we train the way we do today.

The philosophy of karate practice is based upon Zen Buddhism. Whether this is a later Japanese import to help face-lift the image of early karate, or whether it

Above: We are justified in regarding Funakoshi Gichin as the founder of karate as we know it today. He is responsible for changing its emphasis from a method of self defense to a mental and physical discipline.

Right: Kyokushinkai karate has its own form of competition, known as 'Knockdown'. This requires power, stamina and the ability to take punishment.

actually obtained on Okinawa, cannot be said for certain. Whichever is the true explanation, Zen Buddhism does not concern itself with the presence or absence of any godhead. It is solely concerned with gaining the ability to 'see things as they really are'. It teaches that all life involves misery and suffering caused by our continual craving for things, and this craving comes about because we are self interested. Zen Buddhism tries to eliminate this craving and hence suffering, by eliminating the ego.

There are many different ways to achieve this but all involve meditation of one sort or another. This need not be the classical seated meditation of the Zen Buddhist monk – it can occur during the practice of karate, or indeed, during any activity.

At first the student works hard at performing each karate technique correctly. After years of practice, the body performs them without conscious intervention. The opponent attacks; you respond and there is neither fear nor anger to impede your movements. It follows that techniques used in extremes of emotion will not be as effectively applied as those delivered with a calm mind. The most practical techniques in the world are of little use to the person paralysed by fear!

Without this mental detachment, the student of martial art remains a technician; a monkey expertly performing techniques which it does not understand. Unfortunately, the majority of karate exponents are technicians because they have cultivated the physical but ignored the mental.

In conclusion, if one wants to become a true master of karate, then one must train in both the mental and the physical aspects.

The Development of Karate Styles

The early and relatively undocumented history of karate gives only a rudimentary picture of its family tree. More accurate records were not kept until well into the twentieth century. Some work has been done on tracing the early Okinawan lines but researchers keep butting their heads against the lack of written record. We do, however, know that by the early twentieth century, several different forms were thriving (the founding of the Shobukai bears witness to that).

In keeping with traditional martial arts, karate adopted the *ryu* system. Ryu can be translated for our purposes, as 'school'. The school is a core of traditional practice extending back over many generations to the founder. The founder of classic Japanese martial arts typically inaugurated the school following a mystic revelation of some kind. The core teachings of the ryu were subsequently passed on to a small number of selected students and masters succeeded each other through an approved lineage.

However, sometimes there were disputes over who should be the next master. Occasionally senior students found their own interpretations varying too greatly from accepted traditions. In this case they either reviewed their practice, or left to found another ryu.

In an effort to contain the proliferation of schools, the Japanese Karate Federation decided directly to recognise only four major ryu. These are the *Shotokan*, the *Wado Kai*, the *Shito Kai* and the *Goju Kai*. In addition, there is always at least one 'umbrella' group to take the lesser ryu into membership.

Some ryu have arisen relatively recently and so it is possible to give only a short historical account of them. Where this happens, greater coverage has been given to the style's characteristics.

Shotokan

Shotokan karate was originated by the Okinawan schoolteacher and president of the Shobukai, Funakoshi Gichin (1868-1957). As we have seen in the previous section, he was one of the first Okinawan karate instructors to teach on the mainland. Funakoshi was the only student of Master Azato Yasutsune, an exponent of the *shorin ryu* line. The latter could trace his training lineage all the way back to Matsumura Sokon, the student of the military attachés Iwah and Ason. Funakoshi also studied under another shorin ryu master by the name of Itosu Ankoh. Itosu had also studied under Matsumura Sokon, but his other teachers were Shiroma of Tomari and the military attaché, Chinto. Funakoshi too studied for a time under Matsumura Sokon.

At the time of his early training, karate was still shrouded in secrecy and instruction took place in closed gardens, often at night. This, of course, added to its mystique and rumors of karate's effectiveness grew like those of ninjutsu today. Classes were small and limited to the master's children, and close friends of the family. Women, too, were taught and Funakoshi's wife was herself a practitioner. Funakoshi had undoubted ability and this, coupled with his eloquence and literacy, commended him as chairman to the Okinawan Shobukai, despite the fact that more skilled masters were represented thereon.

The easing of restrictions in Okinawa meant that secrecy was no longer necessary and in 1917, Funakoshi gave the first ever public display of karate on the Japanese mainland. He subsequently gave a second display in front of the crown prince, on the latter's visit to Shuri. At the age of 53, Funakoshi resigned from his schoolteaching duties to teach karate full-time. In 1922, he moved permanently to the Japanese mainland.

During 1935, anti-Chinese sentiments influenced him to change the Japanese characters for 'karate'. Although the name was pronounced in the same way, the new characters now meant 'empty hand'. At the same time he changed the names of many of his kata into more acceptable Japanese forms. Two years later, his students succeeded in raising enough money to build a custom-made karate dojo named 'The Shotokan'. This came from the Japanese words *kan*, meaning club and *Shoto*, being Funakoshi's pen-name.

The Shotokan formed the nucleus of influence and development leading to the setting up of the first Japanese karate governing body.

Funakoshi died in 1957 at the age of eighty-nine. He was succeeded as Chief Instructor of the Shotokan by the late Nakayama Masatoshi.

Goju Ryu

Goju ryu was inaugurated by the Okinawan master Higaonna Kannryo (1853-1917). Higaonna was born at Nishimura in the Naha area of Okinawa and trained in the Okinawan fighting art of te. Later he studied under Arakaki Seisho of Kume Mura. One of the Chinese military atachés at Kume Mura was Waishinzan and sources suggest that Higaonna trained under him.

Higaonna subsequently became apprenticed to the trader Yoshimura Udun and made several visits to the Chinese mainland where he came in contact with the Chinese martial arts. He remained in Fukien Province and studied with a master of the Hung style, though some sources claim he also learned *Hsing ye*. If so, no trace of it appears as such in Goju ryu.

Higaonna trained extremely hard and supposedly learned a series of kata in China but, again, if he did, then they do not appear in any of the modern Goju ryu kata. My opinion is that he used moves and techniques taken from Shaolin traditions and incorporated them into his own kata, though it is barely possible, I suppose, that the original Chinese style he learned has since died out.

Higaonna eventually returned to Okinawa and after an intermission, began teaching Naha te karate. His first student and eventual successor was Miyagi Chojun, his second student was Mabuni Kenwa about whom more will be said later. Early training was reputedly monotonous, being no more than weight training plus the kata *sanchin*, repeated over and over again. Many students dropped out through boredom but to those who remained, he taught the core principles of his ryu.

Despite this form of training, Higaonna was reputed to be nimble on his feet, favoring fast techniques. If he taught these to his senior students, then all one can say is that they have changed them since that time.

Miyagi Chojun (1888-1963) was the one to whom he passed custody of his art. Miyagi is responsible for developing naha te into the Goju ryu practised today. He was born in Higashi Machi in Naha and began training under Higaonna when he was fourteen. He persevered with the training and later travelled to China to locate Higaonna's teacher. Miyagi's travelling companion was the naturalised Japanese Yoshikawa, a student of *Peh Hoke* ('White Crane'). Miyagi may have learned some Crane techniques from Yoshikawa but these have been well concealed and are not now clearly evident as such.

Miyagi introduced the kata *tensyo* and made up two elementary kata for teaching to schoolchildren. The core of his training remained sanchin, which he considered an invaluable aid to learning the style. He was fond of the analogy of the willow tree yielding to the hurricane, afterwards returning to its original shape when the wind died down. This is how he felt people should react in karate – yielding to a strong attack but ever ready to snap back.

Miyagi taught karate until he died from a brain haemorrhage at the age of 65. His training was carried on in Japan by his senior student there. Yamaguchi Gogen.

Shito Ryu

It's always helpful to pronounce this style name correctly. The 'i' is almost totally silent, so pronounce it 'shtoe ree yew'. Shito ryu karate was founded by the Okinawan policeman Mabuni Kenwa (1889-1952). He trained under Higaonna Kannryo and Itosu Ankoh. The latter also taught Funakoshi Gichin. These two teachers came from radically different training backgrounds with the result that Mabuni's Shito ryu combines circular techniques with short explosive straight-line strikes, kicks and punches. Further diversity was introduced through Mabuni's training with Master Aragaku of the tomari te school.

Thus Mabuni not only learned the eleven kata of naha

te, he learned a further 40 from the shuri school as well. If this were not more than enough, he then went on to learn a further 45 kata from tomari te. Even so, his appetite for further knowledge was unquenched, so he travelled to China with Miyagi Chojun, posing as a Goju ryu instructor. There he learned a number of Chinese forms and subsequently incorporated them into his style. The kata *haku-cho, pappuren* and *ni pai po* all show clear links with Chinese originals though even here, the movements have been changed and reoriented.

The techniques from all these sources were blended together into a style which he first called *Hanko ryu* ('half-hard school') but then renamed Shito ryu. This latter name comes from the Chinese reading of *'ito'* (from Itosu) and *'higa'* (from Higaonna).

Mabuni was one of the first Okinawans to train mainland Japanese. He taught mainly in the Osaka region and even today, his style remains predominant there.

Mabuni's style allows a great deal of personal interpretation of technique. Thus, a branch line of development occurred through Mabuni's senior student Tani Chojiro. One of Tani's senior students is Kimura Shigeru. Kimura has extensively developed the style and founded a subgroup known as the *Shukokai* ('Way for All'). The Shukokai remains in membership of the parent group, though some of its techniques are markedly different from those taught by the founder.

Wado Ryu

The Wado ryu tradition of karate was founded by the Japanese classical martial artist, Ohtsuka Hironori. Born on 1st June 1892, Ohtsuka began martial training in a version of the *Yoshin ryu* style of jiu jitsu. He achieved teaching grade by the age of only nineteen and specialised in the striking techniques of *atemi*.

Ohtsuka was thirty years of age when he began training under Funakoshi Gichin. He quickly rose through the ranks and was soon regarded as Funakoshi's senior student. However, he greatly admired the *randori* ('free play') of Jigoro Kano's judo and wanted to incorporate this into karate practice. Funakoshi remained adamant that no form of free sparring could be allowed because the techniques of karate were too dangerous. Funakoshi felt that any attempt to make karate into a combat sport would damage its effectiveness as a true fighting art and system of self-improvement.

A tension developed between the two, especially after Ohtsuka pioneered development in early karate competition. Eventually Ohtsuka felt obliged to leave Funakoshi to found his own 'Way of Peace' school. The Wado ryu retains strong links with Shotokan, though both have diverged from Funakoshi's earlier training. There are fewer kata and their names have reverted to the original Chinese titles. Thus the elementary kata of Shotokan - the *heian* – are known by the Chinese name *pinan*.

Ohtsuka's early training in jiu jitsu shows itself in sophisticated body evasions used in response to attack. There is also a return to the more traditional combinations of evasion/block/strike which had been broken up in Shotokan. Some of these include jiu jitsu-type wrist locks and throws. Wado ryu blocks are among the most sophisticated in all karate.

Above: Higaonna Kannryo is regarded as the founder of Goju ryu karate, though many regard his student Miyagi Chojun as having made the greatest contribution to it.

Right: Suzuki Tatsuo (8th dan) demonstrates a kata from the Wado ryu. The black split-skirt (*hakama*) is used by traditional Japanese martial arts.

Kyokushinkai

The 'Way Of Ultimate Truth' was founded by the Korean, Masutatsu Oyama (1923-present). Oyama claims to have trained under Chinese teachers from the age of nine though there is little evidence of any classical influence on his style. He came to Japan in 1938 and trained under Funakoshi Gichin of the Shotokan but left because he felt the style lacked effectiveness. It has been suggested that he trained for a time under Yamaguchi Gogen, the senior Japanese student of Miyagi Chojun. If this is true, then it would explain some rather obvious similarities between the two styles.

Oyama is an outspoken character whose views on the development of Japanese karate have been well documented. He pronounced himself dissatisfied with the styles available to him and set up his own school – the Kyokushinkai. Oyama claims that the principles of his style came to him as a result of two and a half years of virtually solitary meditation in the mountains.

The Kyokushinkai has its headquarters in Tokyo, from where it runs a wide network of schools throughout the world. It is second only to Shotokan in terms of its international organisation and its world championships are among the best attended and most spectacular. One of the reasons for this is the form that Kyokushinkai competition takes.

Oyama sought a form of combat which demanded more from participants than simple agility and speed. His solution was aptly named 'knockdown'. This prohibits punches to the face but allows full power head kicks and techniques to the rest of the body.

The Nature of Karate

Karate is an impact-based fighting system, using obvious muscular effort to accelerate the arms and legs and all styles use the same basic body weapons. The punch typically corkscrews from a palm-upwards to a palm-downwards position on impact, though shorter distance punches sometimes strike with the palm still turned upwards. Middle distance punches can strike with the thumb upwards.

Despite slight differences, all styles of karate use the two largest knuckles. The rationale is that reducing the area through which impact energy is channelled increases its effectiveness. This is also why the side thrusting kick uses the heel and outer edge of the foot rather than the sole. The corkscrew punch, usage of the two knuckles and the heel/foot edge are all characteristic of karate.

Karate is similar to some of the Southern Shaolin long hand boxing styles. These accelerate the fist from near the hip, to a fully extended position with the elbow straightened. The short hand boxing styles use a totally different method of impact development.

Power for karate's punches comes from hip action aided by a rapid pull-back of the non-punching arm. Compare this with the throwing action used in some Chinese systems. The latter use a more relaxed action in which the hips play only a minor role and there is no pull-back of the non-punching fist. Most karate punches are straight line and relatively few use a swinging action.

Karate techniques are focused to deliver their maximum power at a particular point. Energy builds while the fist is accelerating but is quickly shed as the elbow straightens. For maximum effect therefore, the technique must be precisely ranged. The body remains relatively relaxed as the technique accelerates but at the moment of impact, all the muscles tighten and there is a forced exhalation of air. This is vocalised in the form of a shout, or *kiai*. Kiai is a Japanese word which roughly translates out as 'harmony of mind and body'. For our purposes, it means no more than the resolve to hit really hard! Kiai is made from the diaphragm, not from the inter-rib muscles. This gives a deep, penetrating sound. Tommy Morris aptly describes kiai as the sort of grunt one might give when pushing a car.

The body relaxes immediately after the blow has been delivered.

Karate kicks are extremely forceful, though some are vaguely reminiscent of Northern Shaolin snapping kicks. It could be, however, that these are later imports which have been shaped by karate's methods of power delivery. Many kicks use the ball of the foot as impact area, though this is difficult when wearing wooden soled sandals. Certainly the ball of the foot is best employed when barefoot, though what this tells us about the applicability of karate as an everyday fighting system, I'm not quite sure. There are some jumping kicks (that is, kicks made when both feet are off the ground) but compared to Korean and Northern Chinese styles, these are rudimentary and little used.

If the object of karate is to deliver powerful blows and kicks, then it should be possible to do so without the body weapons suffering injury. Body preparation training is an essential part of Chinese martial art and it used to be widespread in karate too, though at a less sophisticated level. However, most schools of modern karate do not now take students through body preparation training. This is because the large numbers training could not all be supplied with the necessary facilities.

When proper facilities are not available, punches and kicks must be aimed into the empty air. This leads to a very serious modification to technique. Picture, if you will, a foot travelling very quickly towards an imaginary target. If the technique is applied with real power, then it will be difficult to halt before the body is pulled off balance. Consequently, the balance is shifted and application of power changes to allow a fast kick that can be retrieved quickly. The problem is that these same techniques are ineffective when applied to a kicking bag.

The way in which karate is taught has had a major effect upon the system in more ways than one. Previously Okinawan karate and traditional Chinese martial arts were taught to only a handful of students through an intimate 'monkey see – monkey do method'. The master was in close attendance and could repeatedly correct each student. Many techniques had no names – and in such an intimate group, there was no need for them anyway! This, however, could not work with larger classes, so the teaching method was altered. What was previously taught as one complex movement was broken down into a series of simpler techniques which could be performed to a count. This had a major effect upon the techniques themselves.

Real-life attacks are very fast and must be countered. The counter might take the form of an evasive movement coupled with a block and strike. However, this would be difficult to teach as one movement to a large class and so the component techniques were uncoupled and taught consecutively. This means that the attack is met first with an evasion and block; then with a strike. While this works well in the training hall, it is too slow in real life.

Karate teaches basic techniques that are quite different from practical forms. The rationale is that this two-tier system makes it easier to learn basic principles which can

then be refined. Unfortunately, the two modes are so dissimilar that there is little transference of learning and where one might have logically expected a technique progression, there is none.

Fundamental changes have also arisen through modifications needed to make free sparring possible. Many students of early karate wanted to spar with each other, though this was sternly prohibited by Funakoshi. Accordingly, a form of 'pseudo-sparring' developed. We would recognise this as prearranged sparring – except that it was performed in real earnest and despite its prearranged nature, injuries were not uncommon. This form of training introduced modifications to the training itself. For example, the semicircular steps used to advance from one stance to another, were deemed too slow, and linear steps took their place.

Finally I would like to consider the credibility of karate's origins by asking whether it is likely that core principles of an ancient tradition were taught to foreigners. The traditional master was always concerned that these treasured principles would fall into the wrong hands and pass outside of the tradition, there to become devalued. If this attitude applied then, as it surely does now, it would be difficult to accept that an Okinawan would be taught the innermost principles of a Chinese tradition. At best he would receive only a rudimentary knowledge.

Taking this supposition further, would Okinawan teachers have taught all they knew to mainland Japanese students? It is a fact that many modern karate teachers withhold fundamental aspects of technique because they always want to keep something in reserve. Has this not always been the case?

These suggestions should encourage us to consider carefully the value of the training imparted to the founders of karate. That there are brilliant karate exponents the world over is not in doubt; but whether karate is as effective a system as it might be is another and more difficult question to be answered.

Above left: All karate styles employ kata as a means of training technique. Funakoshi regarded the performance of kata as the highest expression of karate.

Right: Suzuki Tatsuo (8th dan) is a student of the founder of Wado ryu karate, Ohtsuka Hironori. Suzuki introduced the style to Britain in the mid nineteen-sixties.

Far right: Oyama Masutatsu founded Kyokushinkai karate because he was dissatisfied with existing styles.

KARATE STANCES

Karate places great emphasis upon a strong stance, though 'strong' should not be confused with 'static'. Each stance is correctly balanced, even though it may be held for only a fraction of a second. The stance must be strong enough to withstand an onrushing attack, yet resilient enough to allow a sudden evasive movement. It must also contain within it the potential for an immediate counterattack.

Each stance has two components to consider. The first is its length. This is the distance between the heel of the leading foot and the toes of the trailing foot. Long stances have fore and aft stability, though they are cumbersome

▲ 2

when it comes to explosive advances. Shorter stances are inherently better for faster advances/retreats though they are less suitable for 'digging in' under a direct frontal assault. There is another advantage to the long stance, hitherto unmentioned. That is the isometric training effect it has on the muscles of the upper thigh. This is useful in protecting the knee during powerful kicks.

The second component of a stance is the lateral, or sidestep. Sidestep is the amount by which the heel of the leading foot lies to the side of the toes of the trailing foot. A wide stance gives good lateral stability but it also opens the groin to attack. Stances with wide sidestep lack fore and aft stability. It follows, then, that the most stable general purpose stance has a fair amount of length, plus a little sidestep.

However, the general purpose stance does not of itself give the versatility needed to be able to respond effectively to all manner of attacks. Therefore karate contains a number of specialised stances, momentarily taken up to deal with any particular exigency. Because of their relatively poor general stability, they must be used with caution.

Formal stances have little to do with karate in action. They are used as part of the courtesy ritual which attends practice. The most common is the attention stance which students take up at the beginning of training, when they are listening to instructions. This has neither a length nor a width component because the heels are pressed together while the feet turn outwards. The body is erect and the hands rest open with the palms on the front of the thighs.

Moving to the next stage of readiness, the left foot steps out a half-pace to the left, followed by the right moving a half pace to the right. The hands close into fists (**photo 1**). Note that the shoulders are relaxed and the head is erect. The muscles are relaxed but prepared. Schools such as the Kyokushinkai do not simply clench their fists but move them in intersecting circles across the chest before they come to rest in a 'twenty-to-four' position.

The second type of stance is used for training purposes. However, having said that, I must point out that what is a training stance for one style is a general stance for another. I refer specifically here to the 'hourglass stance'. This is hardly ever used in Wado ryu, occurs infrequently in Shotokan, has a wider usage in Shito ryu and is often employed in both Kyokushinkai and Goju ryu. As we shall shortly see, it is the foundation stance for basic punching and blocking practice. Goju ryu regards it as the core stance.

One final point, before setting out to describe each stance in turn. There is an interesting progression of stance heights between the styles and though this does not hold good for all cases, one can nevertheless generalise and stay that Shotokan stances are the longest and lowest whilst Goju ryu are the shortest and highest.

Wado ryu uses the next longest stances whilst Kyokushinkai and Shito ryu are quite short.

The first stance to be considered is the forward stance and we will consider in detail the Shotokan version of it (**2**). The left foot is a good pace and a half in front of the right and the leading foot faces forward. The front knee is well bent and directly above the mid part of the instep. The rear leg functions as a prop, the knee is locked in the fully extended position and the rear foot turns 45 degrees from straight ahead. The hips and shoulders face square-on to the front. There is a sidestep of at least two fist-widths and the center of gravity is low, making this a very stable stance indeed. The shoulders are relaxed and the head is erect.

The Wado ryu stance is slightly higher and the rear foot is perhaps a little more angled to the front. However, it is worth noting that twisting the foot too far forward increases the tendency for the rear knee to drop. Conversely, not twisting the rear foot enough prevents the hips from turning square-on. Kyokushinkai forward stance (**3**) is about the same length as the Wado ryu version but there are some fundamental differences. The first is that the body is leaning forward slightly – though not so much as to jut the chin forward. The rationale behind this comes from a study of how force is applied – to push a car involves leaning into the pushing action. The second difference is that the front knee advances further over the leading foot. This concentrates weight forward.

This same principle operates in Shito ryu forward stance (**4**) where the leading knee overlies the toes. This is a crucial point in Tani-ha Shito ryu because they consider that if the leading fist remains inside an imaginary line rising up from the leading shin, then the stance will be most efficient at damping recoil. Goju ryu forward stance is actually slightly longer than the Shito ryu version but the knee does not overlie the front foot.

Movement between forward stances uses a gliding motion. Beginning from left forward stance (**2** again), the right foot slides forward, so it brushes past the left (**5**). It continues on a full pace and a half before weight is transferred forward to complete right forward stance. This movement appears deceptively simple but there are a

▲ 3

▲ 4

▲ 5

number of points to watch out for. First of all the rear foot is brought up without any movement of the shoulders. Secondly the knees remain bent throughout, so the head does not bob up and down. Thirdly, body weight transfers forward only as the advancing foot reaches its final position. The shoulders remain relaxed throughout and the arms are still.

Drawing back the front foot by half a pace reduces the length of the stance while maintaining side step. The resultant posture is suitable for unspecialised movements in any direction and so it is commonly used as a free-sparring or competition stance. The Wado ryu stance (6) is of middling length. The front foot turns in slightly to guard the groin – but not so far that it inhibits free movement. The rear foot is twisted forward. Note that both knees are now bent, and weight is carried in the middle of the stance, rather than biased towards the front as in the previous example.

The guard is practical, with the forward fist held well out and in the mid-line of the body. The elbow is flexed 90 degrees and kept close to the ribs – it must not lift out to the side. The leading fist is more or less at shoulder height and held in the thumb-upwards position. The rear guard hand is withdrawn into a fist with the knuckles near the center line of the body. The whole body is turned 45 degrees away from the opponent, so that target opportunities are reduced. Having said that, one should not turn so far away that the rear hand is made unusable. The image is one of readiness and wide-ranging capability.

The Kyokushinkai fighting stance (7) tells us much about the fighting methods of that style! The stance is shorter than Wado ryu's and the leading foot points directly forward. Both knees are bent and weight is equally balanced over both feet. The body is turned away to diminish the target but the guard is held high. The front fist is held closer to the body and level with the eyes. The rear fist is brought up until it covers the chin.

▲ 6

▲ 7

▲ 8

Obviously this leaves a lot of body exposed through it affords greater protection to the face and head. Kyokushinkai karateka train to make their bodies resistant to the effects of hard blows and when one considers that they allow full power kicks to the head, the reason for a high guard takes on new meaning!

The Shito ryu fighting stance (8) is similar to the Wado ryu version except that there is slightly more weight on the front foot. Otherwise the length and hand positions are identical. Shotokan's version (9) is similar to both Wado ryu and Shito ryu except that the knees are bent further, so the stance is lower. The leading hand may be open or closed.

Goju ryu tends not to have a stance specifically designed for sparring. Many stances are used according to the situation but in view of the closer ranges favored by the style, the cat stance is often used. This is a very short stance – the leading foot is a mere half-pace in front of the rear. There is no appreciable sidestep. The front foot faces forward and the rear twists outwards by 45 degrees. Both knees are well bent and almost 90 percent of body weight is supported on the rear foot, the front resting lightly with the heel raised. The guard covers the front of the body and is held in close.

The stance is easier to see when the guarding hands are moved away from the body (10). With the left foot leading it is possible to see how close the knees are together, making a direct frontal attack difficult. There is a tendency to poke the backside out and this must be avoided. The stance is tested by lifting the front foot clear of the floor. It should be possible to do that without having to rearrange weight distribution by more than the smallest amount.

Shotokan cat stance is slightly longer (11). The back foot twists outwards a little more and the leading shin is not vertical. Wado ryu cat stance is similar to the Shotokan version, as is Kyokushinkai's. The latter, however, uses a slight sidestep and the shoulders turn away from

▲ 9

▲ 10

▲ 11

▲ 12

▲ 13

▲ 14

▲ 15

▲ 16

▲ 17

forward facing. Sometimes the stance is so short that the shin inclines back towards the rear foot. Shito ryu returns to the Goju ryu mould, with the leading shin descending vertically and the hips fully forwards-facing (**12**). Note how this is facilitated by twisting the supporting foot.

Extending the leading foot a further half-pace and turning the hips to the side produces back stance in Shotokan and Wado ryu (**13**). Weight distribution changes as the front foot slides forward so it is around 65/35 in the longer Shotokan stance, and 70/30 in the slightly shorter Wado ryu version. The difference is apparent when one compares the two leading legs. In Wado ryu, the shin is closer to vertical and the heel is clear of the mat – as it was in cat stance. The Shotokan leading shin is more angled and the foot is flat on the mat. Shotokan twists the hips more square-on than Wado ryu. This is more obviously seen if you look at the shoulder positions.

Goju ryu and Shito ryu both use a totally different back stance. The Shito ryu version (**14**) is similar to a forward stance except that it is both wider and longer, with feet converging. The head and shoulders are turned to look behind. The Goju ryu version is similar except that the stance is longer but not so wide, and the leading foot does not overlie the toes (**15**). The head is turned to see what lies behind. Kyokushinkai does not use a back stance as such, but relies instead upon a longer version of cat stance (**16**).

Straddle stance has considerable sidestep but no length whatsoever. It is formed by stepping out a pace with the left foot, then a pace with the right. The body sinks down between the feet, so weight is evenly spread.

Some schools have two varieties of straddle stance. The first has the feet only slightly diverging (**17**), the second allows them to splay outwards in line with the thighs. In both cases the back is straight and the backside tucked in. The shoulders are relaxed and the head is erect. The Kyokushinkai straddle stances push the knees outward so they overlie the feet.

Nowhere is this last point more clearly seen than in Shito ryu (**18**). Here you can see a vertical drop from knees to feet. Shito ryu only uses the one straddle stance.

▲ 18

▲ 20

▲ 21

▲ 22

▲ 19

▲ 23

▲ 24

Both Wado ryu versions also have a vertical drop from knees to feet. This feature is not so pronounced in Shotokan. Goju ryu returns to the vertical shin format, with feet splayed widely. The stance used during kata can be extremely low indeed (**19**) – but always the shins remain vertical.

Stepping from one straddle stance to another can be accomplished in a number of ways. The Goju method is to twist the hips forward and step to the leading foot (**20&21**). The right foot then carries on through and the hips twist to face in the opposite direction (**22**). The knees are bent throughout, to avoid bobbing up and down. Wado ryu employs what is called 'scissors stepping'. This begins from a straddle stance (**23**) by bringing the rear foot across the front of the left (**24**). Note that the angle of the hips is changed as little as possible. This

causes a torsional stress to develop in the spine, only to be released when the hips twist around to their new position (**25**). Note that the shoulders only follow the action – they do not initiate it.

Quite an interesting stance is generated by twisting the hips in one direction and shifting the weight forward slightly (**26**). This is the 'immovable stance' of Shotokan and it is peculiar to that style.

If straddle stance is narrowed and one foot is advanced so its heel is in line with the toes of the rear foot, then hourglass stance results (**27**). There is more to it than that, however. First of all the hips are lifted up and tilted forward, so the genitals are protected from a kick between the legs. Then the buttocks are gripped tightly together and the upper legs are stiffened, so body weight is taken on the outside edges of the feet.

▲ 25

▲ 26

▲ 27

▲ 28

▲ 29

▲ 30

▲ 31

▲ 32

▲ 33

▲ 34

Kyokushinkai hourglass stance is very similar (28) except that it is not so wide and the front foot does not turn inwards to such a degree. Goju ryu's foot is almost parallel with the rear foot and the stance is not so wide as the Shito ryu version. Neither Shotokan (29) nor Wado ryu (30) use an hourglass stance as such. The Shotokan equivalent is known as *hungetsu-dachi* because it occurs in the kata named *hungetsu* (*dachi* just means 'stance'). Notice how the knees are driven inwards. This is characteristic of Shotokan and is found in none of the other styles. The feet are virtually parallel and the hips are not lifted up and forward.

The Wado ryu stance is known as *seishan-dachi* since it occurs in the equivalent kata to hungetsu, called *seishan*. The knees revert to a more normal postition and the feet are virtually parallel, though the front does actually twist inwards.

Return to ready stance as described in photo **1** and step out a half-pace with one foot to form the appropriately named 'one foot forward stance'. Both feet are flat on the floor and weight is concentrated over the rear. The front foot faces directly forward and the rear twists outwards by nearly a right angle. Both hips and shoulders are virtually square-on and the head faces the front (31).

Shotokan adopts the same posture except that the hips are twisted away from forward-facing (32). Shito ryu twists the rear foot more to the front so the hips turn square-on. Goju ryu stance is similar to the others but Kyokushinkai has both feet parallel and facing forwards.

One legged stance (sometimes called 'crane on a rock' stance) is transient, being held only for fractions of a second as the front foot is withdrawn from attack (33). Note how the front knee is raised with the foot in a kicking configuration. The arms are gathered across the body. One legged stance does not appear within Goju ryu. In Shotokan, the knee points directly forward and the supporting leg is bent. Wado ryu adopts the same

stance except that the hips are turned away from forwards-facing (34). Shito ryu also turns the hips away from the direction of the pointing knee.

Wado ryu has its own characteristic stance from which the technique known as reverse punch is delivered. This is very similar to forward stance except that the rear hip is twisted forward, causing the front foot to drag outwards and turn in (35). Note how the back foot has turned until it points directly forwards, closing off the groin from direct attack.

▲ 35

▲ 38

▲ 36 ▶ 37

▲ 39 ▲ 40

▲ 41

▲ 42

▲ 43

Karate thrust punches all use what I have described as the pulley principle. This means using the pull-back of the non-punching arm to help power the punch proper. Imagine that a rope is attached to your extended punch. It loops around a pulley and then comes back to the non-punching arm. It follows that as you pull back the non-punching arm, the other will move forward at the same speed over the same distance. This is a crucial point in the development of a karate thrust punch and to develop maximum power, it is necessary to accentuate the role of the pull-back action.

All the styles use a basic form of static punching practice and perhaps the simplest is the single-side punching method used by the Shotokan. It begins from ready stance with a half pace step with first the left foot, then the right. The outside edges of the feet are approximately equal to the width of the shoulders. The left arm is extended and the fingers point forward. The right is pulled back to the ribs in a palm-upwards fist configuration (36). The shoulders are relaxed. On the command, the left hand is pulled back as quickly as possible while at the same time, the right fist is thrust out. If matters are timed correctly, then the two hands pass each other at the midway position.

The pull back/punching action is continued until the right elbow is nearly extended. The left hand clenches into a fist as the extending punch twists into a palm-down configuration (37). There is a moment of intense muscular spasm as the technique completes, then a phase of relaxation follows as the left hand extends once more and the right is re-cocked for the next punch.

There are a few things worth noting about the sequence. The first is that the clenching of the open left hand into a fist adds extra power to the punch. It is not correct to hold the fist tightly clenched all the time because the muscle action involved would slow the punching movement. Therefore the fist is always clenched but not tightly so. It squeezes tightly only at the moment of completion.

The right hip is pulled back very slightly just before the punch is released. Then it twists forward, though there is a slight delay before the arms begin moving. Though the delay is short, it is nevertheless sufficient to load the lateral body muscles with energy. Think of the muscles as a piece of elastic that the hip twist stretches. When stretch reaches maximum, the punch is released.

The shoulders must remain relaxed, so the arm movement is not impeded. They must not hunch up, even during the muscular spasm. The weight of the punching arm pulls the shoulder joint forward, so the back arches slightly. This stabilises the joint and adds a few more inches of range. The full technique involved in the thrust punch can be seen by reference to the Goju ryu sequence that follows. Both fists are withdrawn to the sides (38). Then the right is part-way extended (39). Note how the fist has not begun to rotate and the palm still faces upwards. This is a valid punch in both Goju ryu and Kyokushinkai styles where it is referred to as 'close punch'. The right arm continues to extend and the fist begins to rotate to its final position. On the way it passes through the 'vertical fist'. configuration. Again, this is a valid intermediate range punch. Finally the fist twists fully (40) and the arm is completely extended. Then the leading arm is pulled back, using the pulley principle and the left thrusts out with equal force. Note how the knuckles always lie in the mid-line of the body.

Kyokushinkai uses virtually the same sequence except that the practice stance chosen is the hourglass. The sequence opens with both fists brought into the center line (41), then the left is withdrawn to the hip. The next frame catches the intermediate vertical punch phase (42) before it thrusts into the final configuration (43). The use

◀ 44   ▲ 45

▲ 46

▲ 47

▲ 48

▲ 49

of hip action is clear in this frame. Shito ryu uses a stance similar to Goju ryu's and a distinct hip action supports the punch. Wado ryu practises static punching from a straddle stance but otherwise the procedure is the same as that previously described.

Dynamic punching takes place during advances or retreats. Either way the object is to synchronize punch delivery with momentum generated by the stepping action in such a way that maximum impact results. This is easiest to see in advancing mode. It begins from right forward stance, with the right fist fully extended and the left held against the sides (44). There is a fast step forward, so the left foot slides past the right (45). Note that the extended arm does not waver. The step continues until the left foot leads. The punch begins only as weight settles on to the left foot (46). Leaning in behind the punch gives it extra recoil absorbing capability.

The Shito ryu sequence is virtually identical except that hip action is more pronounced. The punching hip is withdrawn at the starting position and the front knee overlies the toes. The hips twist square-on at the mid-way phase though the arms do not move at all. At the completion of the step, weight transfers forward over the front foot and the non-punching arm is withdrawn. The punching hip then advances behind the hip action.

The Goju ryu sequence is equally explicit, showing one interesting difference from the foregoing. The sequence begins from a left stance (47) but as the right leg advances, it actually moves inwards as well, brushing past the supporting leg (48). Then it continues on diagonally outwards until the correct length and sidestep are achieved (49). Such semi-circular steps are common in Goju ryu but less so in the other styles. The full extent of the advancing step is most clearly seen in the long move-

▲ 50

▲ 51

▲ 52

▲ 53

▲ 54

ment of the Shotokan lunge punch. It begins from right forward stance with the right arm extended diagonally outwards and down (50). The left foot moves forward and in and both knees remain bent throughout. Notice how the non-punching arm never wavers, even during the late stages of the step forward (51). It is only as weight settles that the left fist thrusts forward (52). Wado ryu uses exactly the same action as Shotokan except that the step forward is shorter.

Reverse punch is similar to lunge punch except that the opposite foot and fist lead. Both begin from forward stance with the same arm and leg leading (53). On the command, the right arm withdraws to the waist and the left hip twists forward. The shoulders are released and the left fist thrusts out in a powerful punch (54). Kyokushinkai sequence begins from a right reverse punch with the left foot leading. The step is directly forward and the shoulders remain still (55). As the right foot moves to its final position, the right arm is pulled back and the punch is made with the left (56). Note the forward-leaning characteristic of this style.

Goju ryu uses a pronounced circular step between the

▲ 55

▲ 56

▲ 57

▲ 58

▲ 59

opening stance and the intermediate position with a significant absence of hip involvement at this stage. The foot continues on an outwards arc and the punch is delivered as bodyweight stops moving. Contrast this movement with the pronounced hip involvement of the Wado ryu stylist. Again there is a pronounced semicircular step, but this time the hips twist at least 45 degrees from forwards-facing (57). This cocks the punch so as the hips twist forward, the lateral muscles are stretched and loaded with power. The shoulders remain turned away until the hips have twisted fully and only then do they release and help throw the punch (58). Exactly the same mechanism operates with Shotokan reverse punch.

Wado ryu has its own peculiar version of a low reverse punch in which the stance is wider than usual and forward lean is greatly exaggerated. Weight is biased over the leading foot and the hips twist behind the punching arm. The body leans in one straight line, all the way from heel to punching shoulder, excepting that the head is raised and the gaze directed forward. The heel of the leading foot is in line with the toes of the trailing foot. Movement between stances involves a wide sweeping arc.

Wado ryu also has its own version of the forward leaning lunge punch (59). Notice how, once again, there is a straight line from the trailing heel to the tip of the punching shoulder. The feet are set at near 90 degrees to each other and there is a complete absence of sidestep. The punch is directed to the opponent's face and the non-punching arm is pulled right back against the ribs.

Snap punch is a fast jab made with the leading guard hand. It is practised in two different ways by the five styles. Kyokushinkai and Goju ryu practise it from a static stance. Shito ryu uses either a static or an advancing movement, whilst Shotokan and Wado ryu use it during an advance.

Thus Kyokushinkai begins from an hourglass stance, carrying both fists high and just over shoulder-width apart. The non-punching shoulder withdraws as the right fist starts out towards the target (60). The punching arm then thrusts straight as the left fist guards the chin. Though there is room for a small hip movement, the majority of force is developed by the pulley principle operating through the shoulders. The sudden injection of the shoulder behind the punch adds extra power (61).

The Goju ryu snap punch is also practised from an hourglass stance though there is little evidence here of either shoulder or hip action (62). No pulley action appears and the majority of the power developed comes from a shrugging action of the shoulders.

▶ 60

▲ 61

▲ 62

▲ 63

▲ 64

▲ 65

▲ 66

The Shito ryu sequence operates from a fighting stance and uses a rather obvious and powerful pulley action. It begins by drawing the leading hand back and down. The rear guard hand moves forward at exactly the same time (**63**). Weight shifts over the front leg as the left fist withdraws. This pulley action helps to thrust the right fist back out again (**64**). Though this may seem somewhat roundabout, it is actually very fast indeed. The scope of the movement has been increased for the purposes of clarity.

Shotokan stylists begin from fighting stance, relying upon the shove generated by the bent back leg. The front lifts and slides forward a good half-pace. This injects con-

siderable momentum into the technique. The body leans forward behind the punch and pulley action is harnessed by pulling the rear guard hand back to the ribs (**65**). So here, both pulley action and body movement work together.

The Wado ryu snap punch begins from one foot forward stance. Both fists are carried on the front of the thighs. On the command, the front foot slides forward, using pressure from the rear foot as motive force. Both fists are raised as this is happening (**66**). The fist thrusts into the opponent's face as body movement comes to a stop (**67**). The punching action is powered by the motion of the body and a forward movement of both hands. The

▲ 67

▲ 68

▲ 69

▲ 70

punch is quickly retrieved but the stance is held for a second or so before drawing up the rear foot part way. Then the leading foot withdraws.

Wado ryu also uses a curious variant of the snap punch called 'hip twist snap punch'. This begins in the same manner except that the leading foot inclines inwards during the slide forward (68). The arm movement proceeds as in the previous technique except that the hips twist when the slide comes to a stop. This slews the rear foot around, so the karateka lies at an angle to the imaginary opponent, instead of square-on (69). The fist is retrieved, there is a short pause, and starting stance is resumed once more.

Hammerfist is a clubbing attack which uses the little finger-edge of the closed fist. It is delivered with either a vertical or horizontal circular action. The first examples are vertical applications and the last two show horizontal ones. Thus, Shito ryu begins from an hourglass or straddle stance. The left hand is extended across the body with the palm turned downwards. The right is closed into a fist and raised high above the head (70). The left hand draws quickly back and by means of the pulley principle, the right is simultaneously brought sharply down on the target (71) (*overleaf*).

Note that both arms follow curving paths since one straight and one curved movement would be difficult to

▲ 71 ▲ 72 ▲ 73 ▲ 74

synchronise in terms of power. Note also that the right hip advances behind the blow, and that the left hand closes into a fist even as the right brakes to a stop. If the knees are bent slightly at the same time, then the center of gravity is shifted and additional force is made available.

The Wado ryu hammerfist can be used to break a grip. Thus forward stance is withdrawn into a cat stance, pulling the seized arm close into the body (72). The forearm is drawn up the front of the body (73) and then the fist is brought sharply across and down (74). This action is short and sharp. The shoulders shrug as the hammerfist completes.

Goju ryu uses a large circular movement that takes the arm from well over the head, down on to the target. The momentum of the moving arm is important and power is localised there, with no additional hip or pulley action taking place.

Kyokushinkai hammerfist shown here is of a horizontal kind. It begins from a cat stance with the right fist in position against an imaginary opponent's temple (75). The left arm draws back hard against the ribs. The right

fist drops and moves back to the chest, so the elbow points directly forward. At the same time, the left fist is brought up and behind the head, stretching the muscles of the chest (76). The right arm is drawn strongly back and the left swings around in a wide arc, powered by a straightforward pulley action. Even as the right fist comes to a stop, so the left fist brakes to a stop on the imaginary opponent's temple (77).

Shotokan hammerfist demonstrated in the following sequence reverses the circular action described above. Beginning from a low straddle stance, the right arm wraps closely against the chest as the left extends forward (78). This is to generate the pulley action needed to help power the strike. The left fist draws back strongly and the right smacks horizontally into the opponent's ribcage (79).

Though I have selected only one hammerfist from each of the styles, the reader should not gain the false impression that each style uses only this particular technique. In fact each style uses hammerfist in many different ways. The same comments apply to the next technique too.

▲ 75 ▲ 76 ▲ 77

▲ 78

▲ 79

▲ 80   ▲ 81   ▲ 82

Backfist uses the upper surface of the two major knuckles to deliver a circular strike to the side of the opponent's head, bridge of nose, groin, or ribs. In the first example, Kyokushinkai demonstrates a rearwards striking backfist. It begins from a right hourglass stance with the right fist above the left. The head is turned to see the target and the right hand draws around and back, allowing the left to follow it (**80**). The striking action continues by allowing the shoulders to swing fully, so the fist strikes the opponent's ribs (**81**). Here the motive force comes from an unimpeded shoulder action plus the muscles of the striking arm.

The Shito ryu version uses a similar action except that the elbow is bent rather more, so the strike unrolls out and snaps into the target. Point your right elbow at the target, then raise your left arm to the same height. The hips whiplash and fling the arm out on a loose elbow joint and into the target (**82**). The muscles of the arm play a smaller role in generation of force compared to the previous example but the hips take on a proportionately larger role.

The Shotokan version begins from forward stance with the right arm extended and the left resting little finger down on the right shoulder (**83**). The right arm is pulled back strongly, all the way to the ribs. At the same time, the left arm lashes out in a horizontal strike (**84**). Note how the hips twist in the opposite direction to the strike. This might, at first, be thought to rob the backfist of power but actually it speeds the strike up and considerably adds to its range. How could this be so? The shoulder of the striking arm has moved to the front, so half the width of the chest is added to the length of the arm. This explains why a backfist can be used in a situation where reverse punch is out of range.

The Wado ryu backfist uses no pulley action at all but relies solely upon the unrolling action described in the above example. Typically the basic strike is delivered from one foot forward stance with both fists carried low on the front of the thighs. Weight shifts entirely over the front foot and the right elbow rises to point at the opponent (**85**). The hips twist away from the eventual strike. In the final position, the striking arm extends fully, the hips are turned away and there is virtually no weight on

the rear leg. The body leans forward to get maximum range.

Wado ryu backfist is delivered with a relaxed wrist, so it trails slightly as the arm extends but whiplashes forward when arm movement brakes to a stop. The technique is delivered with a snappy action characteristic of the style.

Goju ryu backfist is here demonstrated in a vertical format, aiming at the bridge of the opponent's nose. It begins from hourglass stance with both fists held high in front of the body. The striking arm lashes into the target, assisted by a forward movement of the shoulder (**86**). The whole thing is quite short range and extremely powerful. A similar action is used when the basic Kyokushinkai backfist is delivered to the side or front. It begins from an hourglass stance with both fists brought together in front of the chest (**87**). The right fist arches up in a semicircle, striking the imaginary opponent on the bridge of the nose (**88**). This is the simplest form of backfist, since it uses only the energy generated in the striking arm.

Knife hand is generally used with a circular action though there is one exception to this, as we shall see. The fingers are fully extended and the thumb locks across the palm of the hand. Impact is made with the ridge of muscle running between the base of the little finger and the wrist. Accurate usage is needed to ensure that you do not strike with the base of the little finger (painful!), or the wrist itself (also painful!). There is a tendency for the fingers to rattle together, so they should be momentarily stiffened on impact. As we shall see, some styles slightly cup the hand.

The easiest to follow is the Kyokushinkai horizontal knife strike, performed from an hourglass stance. The left elbow points forward and the hand is brought near to the right shoulder. The right hand raises behind the head, with fingers extended (**89**). The left arm is strongly pulled back, using the pulley principle. This helps draw the right arm around in a circular movement (**90**). Notice how the fingers point upwards. As the left hand comes to rest against the ribs, so the right brakes to a stop against the imaginary opponent's neck. The hand position changes sharply during the last few centimeters of

▲ 83

▲ 84

▲ 85

▲ 86

▲ 87

▲ 88

▲ 89

▲ 90

▲ 91

▲ 92

▲ 93

▲ 94

▲ 95

▲ 96

▲ 97

movement. It is delivered with a slightly cupped palm which faces upwards (91) (*page 39*). This imparts a scooping action to the strike.

The Wado ryu sequence shows the same type of movement except that an obvious hip involvement is added to the pulley action. A forward lean gives extra range. The sequence begins from a left fighting stance in which the left arm has dropped in a deflection move. The right hand is extended out from the body (92). Both hands are turned palm-downwards. The left hand is then strongly withdrawn to the ribs as the hips rotate behind the strike. The right hand swings around and rotates palm-upwards as it nears the target (93). Note how far the shoulder is involved, so range is dramatically increased.

Goju ryu uses a characteristically wide circle in which to generate power and, in the example chosen, the strike is made from a low straddle stance. The right hand guards the chest as the left circles over the top of the head, cutting down on to the opponent's collar bone (94). Power is generated by acceleration through the long movement involved. In general terms, circular techniques are more effective from short ranges because they allow acceleration over a longer distance than is available to a linear strike.

The Shito ryu knife hand example chosen shows a completely different application to what has gone before insofar as it is delivered with a straight thrusting movement, attacking the opponent's shoulder joint and upper arm. It begins from forward stance, with the right arm fully extended and the left hand palm-upwards against the ribs. The left hip twists forward but the arm remains where it is, so the lateral muscles are stretched. Then the left shoulder releases and the left arm thrusts forward. As this is happening, the right arm is withdrawing at equal speed. The strike is delivered with the little finger edge of the left hand (95).

Ridge hand uses the thumb-edge of the hand to strike at the opponent's temple, jaw, neck and groin. All the major styles use it and a swinging, circular action is the most common method of delivery. The Shotokan version shown attacks the side of the neck via a rising circular strike delivered from forward stance. The left arm is dropped down in front of the groin and the hips are

▲ 98

turned away from forwards-facing. The rear hand is closed into a fist. The right hip twists forward and the left hand pulls back to the hip. A combination of these two actions provides power for the strike which curves out from the ribs and into the target. The first suddenly unclenches just before impact is made (96).

Shito ryu has a comparable strike delivered from forward stance. This time the non-striking arm is extended with the palm turned upwards. The striking arm drops diagonally down across the body and the hand is turned palm-downwards. There is a double movement of the hip coupled with strong pull-back of the left hand. This powers the strike as it circles up and into the target (97).

The Goju ryu example is of a horizontal strike delivered without obvious hip or shoulder action. It begins from a palm-downwards position, the other hand acting as a guard across the chest. Then the striking arm curls around in a horizontal strike to the opponent's floating ribs (98).

42

▲ 99   ▲ 100   ▲ 101

▲ 102   ▲ 103   ▲ 104

Ridge hand is also useful against the groin, as this next version from Kyokushinkai shows. It begins from a forward stance with the leading arm extending diagonally downwards. The hand is held palm-downwards just above the knee. The other is withdrawn to the ribs (**99**). The rear hip twists forward slightly and the leading hand withdraws at the same time, so the striking hand curls forward with the elbow bent and rotates palm downwards as contact is made (**100**).

The Wado ryu version of a groin strike is even more simple. It too begins from a forward stance but this time the non-striking arm is held in front of the face as a guard. The striking arm trails. A pronounced hip action drives the ridge hand vertically upwards and into the groin (**101**). No pulley action is possible because face guard must be maintained so close to the opponent. Power comes from both hip and shoulder action.

The final group of hand techniques to examine are the elbow strikes. These are powerful short range strikes using the tip of the elbow. Contrary to what you might expect, it is difficult to catch the funny-bone and efforts should be made to avoid wasting impact energy by striking with the forearm.

The first application is a short range horizontal strike used by the Goju ryu. Starting position is a cat stance with both arms held across the chest. Weight shifts backwards over the rear leg as the non-striking arm is pulled back to the ribs. This provides power for the horizontal elbow strike (**102**). Note the forward lean to concentrate power.

The Shito ryu version uses a rather more obvious hip movement. The technique begins from forward stance with the hips twisted 45 degrees away from square-on. The hip is then driven forward as the leading arm is

▲ 105

▲ 106

pulled back. This generates sufficient speed and power to wipe the elbow across the opponent's jaw in a horizontal arc (**103**).

A slightly different version is demonstrated by the Wado ryu. Here the opening is made from a straddle stance with the leading arm extended. This makes for an even greater usage of the hip than the previous example. The hips twist strongly, changing the straddle into a forward stance. At the same time, the leading hand pulls strongly back as the striking elbow swings into an uppercut to the opponent's jaw (**104**). Maximum power is generated only when the striking arm and leading leg are on different sides of the body.

The Shotokan example shown begins from a straddle stance. The striking arm is drawn across the body and the other fist is held palm-upwards against the ribs (**105**). The striking arm thrusts into the opponent, using the palm of the other hand to augment the movement (**106**). A slight lean into the target adds power and helps dissipate recoil.

The final elbow strike shown is the descending version. This is applied from straddle stance, with the nonstriking arm extended across the front of the body. The other arm reaches above the head. Pulley action powers the strike as the non-involved arm pulls back to the ribs. The elbow drops directly down on to the back of the opponent's neck (**107**) and further power is gained by slightly flexing the knees. This must be done just as the elbow is about to connect.

▲ 107

KARATE KICKS

▲ 108

If Southern Shaolin styles of kung fu played a major role in the development of karate, then we would expect kicks to be fairly rudimentary and confined to below-waist thrusting actions, striking with the heel or sole of foot. When we consider historical documents about early practice, we do, in fact, see that kicks were of this type. It was said of Funakoshi that he only ever used straight kicks, and then to below-waist targets.

The modern form of karate uses many highly effective kicks. How has this come to be? My own theory is that the karate of Funakoshi's era was essentially a close-range fighting system, where standing on one leg was not to be recommended. However, when the twin aspects of sparring and combat sport developed, distances between combatants increased and kicks provided a means of bridging that distance without bringing the body into the opponent's punching range.

If this is so, then circular and high kicks have been imported from other sources. Northern Shaolin martial art is known for its kicking techniques but what contact, if any, did the Japanese have with this region of China and how likely were Chinese masters to teach foreigners their traditions? Furthermore, if the high/circular kicks of

▲ 109

karate came from Northern Shaolin, how come they appear so much more effective than their antecedents?

A possible answer to both of these questions is that the Northern Shaolin source has come into karate through the back door. By that I mean through Korea, where the Northern influence and Korean inclinations resulted in the development of really effective circular/high kicks. For example, the reverse roundhouse kick was unknown to high ranking Japanese teachers in Britain during the early sixties and it is not to be found in the syllabus of any style during that period.

The first time it was seen in public by Britons was through a photograph of Kono Teruo of the Wado Kai performing it. At first the photograph was mistaken for a poor high side kick. I say 'poor' because if it was a side kick, then Kono was making the basic mistake of kicking with the sole of his foot. In fact he was performing a reverse roundhouse kick and within a year or two, this mysterious technique had reached Britain.

Karate and Korean martial art clubs nestle cheek by jowl in many American towns. Indeed I have seen tae-kwondo and tang soo do clubs describe themselves as 'karate', since that is the name of the brand-leader. Americans went into multi-style competition at an earlier date than practitioners in Europe and magazines of the period depict matches between Korean tang soo do and Japanese karate. Such events would have been an ideal place for techniques to be seen and appraised by others.

Thus I propose that the circular/high kicks were imported from the Korean systems between the thirties and sixties. As a quick check, I looked at the most traditional of the styles covered by this book – Goju ryu – and noted that they do not appear to practise (in a formal sense) the reverse roundhouse kick. They appear to rely more on low thrusting kicks, though this is not, of course, to say that they do not practise techniques such as roundhouse kick to the head. It's just that the emphasis is elsewhere.

This study examines four principal kicking techniques only. These are the front kick, the side kick, the back kick and the roundhouse kick. Each style performs them in a more or less similar manner except for the Tani ha Shito ryu group. The latter has introduced a number of fascinating changes based upon their notion of power development.

All kicks in karate use a rapid pull-back of the spent technique, both to avoid it being seized by the opponent and to restore both feet quickly to the ground. This means that the kicking action is accomplished by the knee. Thus there is an active phase of acceleration as the foot is pulled from the floor and the kicking knee swings forward and up. Then there may be a passive phase in which the upper leg brakes to a stop, allowing the knee joint to snap the kick out. Obviously these two phases must be exactly synchronized if power is to be conserved. Sometimes the passive phase is omitted in favour of active lower leg extension.

We begin with front kick which, as its name implies, travels more or less in the direction that the hips are facing. Impact is made with the ball of the foot, so the toes must be pulled back. Initially this leads to problems because the muscle action needed to do that interferes with the speed and range of the kick. The coach of the British team advises students to relax their toes, and to kick with the heel low, so the toes flex back of themselves upon impact.

The first pre-requisite of a good front kick is to raise the front knee high, while keeping the shoulders relaxed and the arms still. This is clearly seen in the basic Shoto-kan version (108). Notice that the supporting foot is twisted slightly outwards and the knee is bent. The active raising of the knee flows seamlessly into the lower leg extension, so acceleration is continuous throughout the kick (109). The arms remain virtually motionless during delivery and body weight is biased over the supporting foot. This is important because the moving foot possesses considerable momentum and if this is not counterbalanced, the body will fall forward after the spent kick.

The Wado ryu front kick is very similar except that there is more hip action. The knee is raised as before but it drops slightly as the kick impacts (110). This is an essential part of the thrusting action of a good front kick and .when it is missing, the foot simply skates up the front of the target. Actually the path which the foot follows is quite complicated. It is lifted with the sole parallel to the mat and having reached the required height, it proceeds more or less directly into the target. It does not, as many people seem to think, simply swing upwards. The hip plays a major role in development of this thrusting action. It moves from a withdrawn rearward position to a forward attitude and not only does this favor the thrusting action, it also adds half the width of the hips to the kick's range.

▲ 110

▲ 111

This is clearly seen in the Kyokushinkai front kick. The hip is fully withdrawn in fighting stance but as it moves forward, you can clearly see the supporting leg twisting outwards and the kicking hip advancing (111). Foot rotation continues even as the kick is being thrust out. Note that the knee does not drop during kick delivery. This is because the lower leg is actively propelled out by the action of the upper leg muscles.

The Tani ha Shito ryu group uses a novel way of developing power based upon a series of linked muscle actions. Firstly the body arches, so the muscles on the front of the stomach and thighs are pre-stretched. The energy inherent in this action helps spring the heel of the kicking foot clear of the mat (compare the Wado ryu parallel lift-off). The hips twist powerfully, stretching the upper thigh muscles as the lower leg lags slightly behind (112). Note how far the kicking knee has been thrust forward by hip action. The stretched upper thigh muscles then behave like elastic bands, contracting quickly to thrust the lower foot into the target. Additional power is injected by further stretching the stomach muscles with a pronounced backwards lean – though the head should never lean back too far (113).

Thus the delivery path is quite different from the Wado ryu method. Shito ryu front kick travels in a diagonal path from floor to target while the other describes almost a parabola.

Goju ryu provides an example of how cat stance can be used for thrusting a short-range front kick into the opponent's stomach. The cat stance must first be set up correctly so the front foot can be lifted without giving any tell-tale warnings. The knee swings quickly to kicking height, and notice that the sole is parallel to the mat (114). Because the kick does not benefit from the acceleration offered by a long action, it derives all of its force from an active thrusting out of the lower leg (115). Notice that the shoulders remain relaxed and the guard is effective.

One step front kick is used when the distance to be covered exceeds the length of the leg. In practice, slight increases in range can be gained by allowing the supporting leg to slide forward, pulled by the action of the extending kick. This, however, is quite a sophisticated action and is only available to those skilled enough to be able precisely to control the center of gravity. When a slide is insufficient, a step forward provides the answer.

▲ 112

▲ 113

▲ 114

▲ 115

Once again we encounter the 'scissors step'. The sequence begins from a normal fighting stance and the rear foot slides forward and sets down in front of the erstwhile leading foot. Note that it is already twisted outwards in preparation for the following kick (**116**). The kick then follows (**117**). The step must be made quickly, otherwise the opponent is alerted and can take evasive action. Also the knees must be kept bent throughout, or

the head will bob up and down. Length of the step varies according to the distance to be covered.

Skilled exponents skip forward, raising the kicking knee even before the new supporting leg effectively touches down. This cuts technique time dramatically and adds moving body momentum to the power of the kick.

The side kick is so named because the hips are turned

▲ 116

▲ 117

▲ 120

▲ 121

▲ 118

▲ 119

away from the direction of the thrust and impact is made with the outer edge of the foot and heel. There are two varieties of the kick, one delivered with an upwards snapping action, the other performed with a thrusting movement.

Side snap kick is practised by the Shotokan from a straddle stance. The kick is set up once again by a short scissors step that takes the rear foot across the front of the supporting leg. This point is important and will be referred to again later. The kicking knee is then raised high against the chest (118). The kick takes the form of an up-swinging arc that catches the opponent in the throat or under the jaw (119).

As in all scissors steps, the knees remain bent throughout and the advancing foot is twisted in preparation for the kick. The knee is raised high because the kick is otherwise strictly limited. If the knee is not raised sufficiently, then kicking height is reduced. Notice that the hips are turned sideways-on and the body leans slightly away from the kick. The foot weapon is formed by lifting the big toe while depressing the others.

Side thrust kick is practised by all five styles and it is quite different to the snap kick. The Goju ryu version is demonstrated from cat stance and begins when the front foot is drawn back and up. The correct foot position is adopted, then the supporting foot twists as the kicking heel is driven diagonally down on to the opponent's kneecap (**120**). The kick is powered by two quite different actions. The most obvious is simply the straightening of the bent knee. The less obvious but very important action lies in the way that the hips swivel away from the kick itself from forward facing to diagonal facing. In practice the two actions occur simultaneously, though the thrust of the lower leg does tend to pull the hips around.

This combination hip twist/thrust action is also seen in the Wado ryu version where the rear foot of a fighting stance is raised and brought forward. The rising knee moves diagonally across the chest, causing the hips to turn away from the target (**121**). The foot is correctly formed at this point and the heel is pointing in the direction of the target. The lower leg is then thrust out in a rising action (**122**). Notice how the upper body leans back to counterbalance the kick, the head raised enough to sight along the front of the body. One arm is extended above the kicking leg; the other folds across the chest as a guard. The supporting leg has swivelled so far that it is pointing diagonally backwards. This is a characteristic of side thrust kick and shows how far the hip is involved in the action.

The basic side kick can also be performed from a sideways-facing position by means of a scissors step. In contrast to the step used to set up side snap kick, this time the advancing foot skims behind the supporting leg (**123**). This change is necessary to set the hips up for the thrusting action. Stepping across the front of the supporting leg actually impedes hip action. As the stepping heel sets down, the kicking foot lifts from the floor and travels in an upwards diagonal to the target (**124**). Here too the body leans back and the hips are fully twisted away from the kicking action. Length of step is adjusted to suit the distance from target and skilled exponents use a flat, skipping advance to cover distance quickly.

Kyokushinkai uses a very similar sequence except here the starting position is a fighting stance. The advancing

▲ 122

▲ 123

▲ 124

▲ 125

▲ 126

▲ 127

▲ 128

▲ 129

leg steps behind the supporting leg to set the hips up for the kick (125) and the kicking foot lifts off with no hesitation (126). This time, though, it is not simply thrust into the target. Instead it rises close to the supporting leg, after which it thrusts out and down into the target (127). As before, the body leans back and the hips twist away.

In all of the previous cases, the kick has been delivered with the heel and edge of foot. However, Shotokan uses an alternative version which is intended to glance across the opponent's body. The little toe part of the foot actually leads and slices across the opponent's ribs with a cutting action.

The other version of the Shotokan thrusting kick is interesting in that it uses a scissors step to take the stepping foot across the front of the supporting leg (128). This then calls for a complete turning action of the hips to set the kick up (129). The rationale here is that the extra hip action provides a bonus in power.

In many ways, side thrust kick and back kick are similar. Both use a degree of hip rotation and a thrusting action to drive the heel of the foot into the target. The Wado ryu version begins from a fighting stance (130) by sliding the front foot across and twisting on it so the back is turned to the opponent (131). The kicking foot then lifts and is thrust back into the opponent's mid section (**132**).

There are a number of interesting points to take up about this kick. The first is that the degree of opening side step determines the direction in which the kick will travel. Too much, or too little sends the kick to either side of the target. The head does not turn to view the opponent, so an accurate placing is essential. Secondly, skill is needed to step and turn quickly without losing balance. This is essential because standing with your back to the opponent is not recommended! Thirdly, hip rotation has to stop at the right moment, or the kick will be off-target. The body leans forward to counterbalance the kick and the arms are held close to the sides. Impact is made with the heel, and the foot is inclined as close to vertical as can be managed. Fourthly, the set-down involves a sharp turn to face the opponent again. This means retrieving and precisely placing the spent kick so that when the turn occurs, the resulting fighting stance has the required degree of sidestep.

Shito ryu uses a short spinning action over the front

▲ 130

▲ 131

▲ 132

foot from a fighting stance during which the kicking foot is lifted (133). The body is oriented by means of the opening spin, so skill is needed to ensure accuracy. Like the Wado ryu version, the head is turned away so it is not possible to correct for changes in the opponent's position once the kick has started. The foot thrusts directly backwards, the body leaning forward to counterbalance the weight of the extending leg (134). Note that the supporting leg has twisted completely away from the opponent and the kicking knee is directed to the floor.

The Shotokan back kick uses a similar turning motion from a forward stance but the eyes continue to regard the opponent (135). The kicking leg is raised and the head rotates to look over the shoulder (136). The heel of the kicking foot is then thrust out into the target (137). The eyes remain on the target at all times.

Kyokushinkai also uses a turning motion of the front foot to set the angle up correctly. As with Shotokan, the eyes are kept on the target at all times. The kicking knee is raised (138) and thrust into the target (139). The whole action is accomplished smoothly, with a gradual acceleration throughout the technique.

▲ 133

▲ 134

▲ 135

▲ 136

▲ 138

▲ 137

▲ 139

Goju ryu uses this same turning motion, but this time from a straddle stance (**140**). The front foot turns and the rear draws to it as the head turns to view the opponent (**141**). The kicking knee is then raised and thrust diagonally down into the opponent's kneecap or groin (**142**).

Roundhouse kick is a completely different type of kick to any of the foregoing. It is a circular, or turning kick in which the foot describes a horizontally biased arc into the target. The supporting foot always twists to allow the hip on the kicking side to advance and there are varying degrees of body lean according to style. Impact is made with either the ball of the foot, or with the instep. In the latter case, the strike is made with the base of the shin and front of the ankle rather than the foot blade itself.

Perhaps the most clear cut roundhouse kick available for study is that used by the Shotokan. Starting position is a forward stance, with the arms held relaxed at the sides. The kicking foot is raised sharply to the side until the knee is at the correct height for kick delivery (**143**). The supporting leg then twists as the kicking hip swivels forward and as the knee comes to point at the target, so the lower leg is snapped out and the ball of the foot impacts (**144**).

The most difficult thing to get right is the height of the kicking leg. If it is not high enough, then the resulting kick is low and attempts to elevate it lead to a poor hip position and loss of impact. It must be possible to reach the required height easily because there is no pause in the action once the foot is raised from the mat. The hips must swivel smoothly, so the kick curves across the front of the body. Note that the kick is almost horizontal throughout its arc; there is little upwards movement.

The Shito ryu version is a shortened version of the same action. If begins from a fighting stance but the foot is raised diagonally up, so the knee crosses the body to act as a fender against sudden attacks (**145**). Then the lower leg curves horizontally into the target, striking with the shin/instep (**146**). The Tani ha Shito ryu version arches the back to help pull the foot from the mat and the hip action is such that the kicking hip rolls up and over the top of the supporting leg. The body leans back to

▲ 140

▲ 141

▲ 142

▲ 143

▲ 144

▲ 145

counterbalance the action and the supporting leg twists right around.

The Wado ryu version is very similar, with the knee arching across the front of the body and the shoulders leaning back. Note that an effective guard is maintained throughout the kicking action. The hip continues to swivel throughout the kick and the supporting leg twists until it is almost facing backwards (**147**).

The Kyokushinkai version is mid-way between the Shotokan and Shito ryu/Wado ryu models in that the knee comes across the front of the body during the early stages of the kick. The body leans well away and the kicking hip rolls over the top of the supporting hip. In Goju ryu roundhouse kick can be delivered with the front foot from a cat stance. Hip action is more restricted as there is a shorter distance over which to accelerate the kick. Nevertheless, the knee points at the target and is raised sufficiently to allow a horizontal trajectory.

▲ 146

▲ 147

BLOCKING TECHNIQUES

▶ 148

▲ 149

▲ 150

▲ 151

Blocking techniques combine with body evasions to cause an attack to be deflected. Sometimes body evasion alone is sufficient to cause the technique to miss and the block functions simply as insurance. Other times the block itself forms part of the counter attack, closing off the opponent and preventing the immediate launch of a follow-up attack. The block can itself be the attack insofar as it injures the opponent.

The kinetics of the block are that it should take the opponent's technique and redirect it, so it misses the target it was aimed for. How this is achieved will vary according to the block used. Some blocks reach out for the incoming attack, meet it at an angle and redirect it past its target. These need a high level of skill but only a low level of physical strength. Other blocks literally smash into the attacking technique. This requires less skill but more physical strength. Bear in mind that the moving leg develops more kinetic energy than the arm; besides which its bones are stronger. It therefore makes sense not to meet a kick square-on with your block.

The mechanics of blocks vary according to their purpose. Deflecting blocks go for maximum leverage, catching the attack near the wrist/ankle, where the minimum of energy produces the maximum of deflection. Smashing blocks use a large circular movement, perhaps aided by a pulley action and hip twist. Some swing both arms in unison in what is called an 'augmented block'. Such blocks are not necessarily applied to the extremities but can strike the elbow or knee joints instead.

High-level blocks contain within themselves the next attack. Thus the Wado ryu hip twist snap punch that we discussed two chapters ago meets the incoming punch at an angle. The attack is deflected and the punch goes on into its target. Typically such blocks are specific in their application; that is to say they sweep only a small vector clear. If cues are misread and the wrong response used, then the block may well prove ineffective. Less skillful blocks sweep a whole area clear of techniques and work equally well with a whole range of attacks.

The block itself should contain the minimum number of moves and require the smallest possible movement if it is to be effective in the ordinary practical sense of the word. Pulley actions and large blocks tend to work well at basic training level but they are simply too slow to use in a fighting situation.

Timing is of the essence when applying a block. A technique has relatively low kinetic energy when it begins and so can be easily blocked. The Shito ryu thrusting knife hand is ideal for this purpose. It can completely defeat an incipient attack if aimed early on into the attacking shoulder. The level of energy is also low after the attack has missed and is being retrieved. Maximum energy is developed mid-way through the attack's execution, so at that point only the strongest karateka should apply direct-acting blocks.

Distance too is of importance. The maximum power developed by a technique occurs at its extremity, so any block that contacts the ankle or wrist must be prepared for this. On the other hand, a block which deflects the elbow or knee need not be so robust. The block's direction is a third consideration, and we have touched briefly upon this above. A block can move in the opposite direction to the attack, so there is a head-on collision between the two. The block can also strike the attack at a right angle, so the latter is slapped off course. This requires

less violence. The third method is to apply the block at an angle to the attack. This requires the least violence. Remember that all blocking is active; that is, you never leave your block passively in the path of the attack. Always go out to meet the attack, applying the block in such a way as to obtain the maximum effect with the least amount of movement or effort.

The first block to be considered is the head block. This uses the forearm in an upwards rolling movement that bumps an incoming punch over the head. To succeed, it must get to the punch before the latter gets to the face! Secondly it must lift the punch sufficiently, so it clears the head and does not simply smack into the forehead. Thirdly it must intercept the incoming punch far enough away to allow the deflection to succeed.

Goju ryu head block begins from an hourglass stance with the right hand pulled back to the hip and the left extended upwards. The blocking fist is well above the head and twists until the little finger points upwards (148). The blocking arm is then withdrawn down and close to the chest, where it is overlaid with the non-blocking arm in the form of an 'x' (149). A pulley action then ensues, with the spent blocking arm drawing back to the ribs as the new block rises upwards (150). Note the forearm rotation which takes place between photos 149 & 150. This strengthens the block and increases the deflection obtained. A corresponding rotation occurs in the withdrawing arm. Note also that the crook in the elbow is close to the side of the head, so decreasing the opportunity for leverage to jam the forearm down and into the head.

The Kyokushinkai head block is very similar, though notice that the blocking forearm is turned palm-downwards. As in the previous sequence, the blocking arm is drawn down close to the chest where the other forearm overlays it. The pulley action then continues with the new blocking arm rising to the final position as the other comes to rest against the ribs (151). Lack of rigidity in the forearm is compensated for by injecting the shoulder and hip behind the block.

Shito ryu block is demonstrated from a fighting stance. The lead hand drops down and across the stomach as the rear hand moves forward over the top of it (152). This sets up the pulley action needed to power the block. The extended arm is then strongly withdrawn and the head block rolls up the front of the body, coming to its final position with the little finger turned upwards (153).

▲ 152 ▲ 153

▲ 154

▲ 155

▲ 156

▲ 157

Notice that the block leans away from the head so an extra safety margin is incorporated. Any head block that allows itself only a couple of inches to deflect a punch clear of the head is cutting things fine! Note also that the forearm is inclined upwards at an angle, so a powerful downwards blow slides off the forearm, rather than meeting it full-on.

The basic Shotokan head block uses a substantial pulley action to power it. It begins from a forward stance, in this case with the leading arm barring downwards above the knee (154). The back foot slides forward and the extended arm moves to point diagonally upwards (155). As the step continues, the raised arm is drawn back down against the body and as this happens, the new blocking arm crosses the front of it (156). The forward movement completes and the blocking arm thrusts upwards as the withdrawing arm settles against the ribs (157). Note that the withdrawing hand twists palm-upwards and closes

▲ 158

▲ 159

▲ 160

tightly into a fist exactly as the blocking forearm rotates little finger upwards.

The Wado ryu block uses a minimum of movement with little pulley action. The block is intended as a deflection rather than a square-on meeting of arms, so a great deal of power is not actually needed. In the sequence shown, the karateka is turning to face the opponent. She has begun from a forward stance and glancing over her shoulder, slides her back foot across. The blocking arm is held low across the stomach, little finger turned inwards. The hips twist powerfully into the turn and the blocking arm travels diagonally up and across the body (**158**). The body's center of gravity moves forward slightly to inject extra power into the action.

Lower parry is a very common basic block used against a variety of straight attacks to the lower stomach. Blocking agent is the forearm, which wipes diagonally down across the front of the body and comes to rest above the leading knee and slightly to the outside of it. The block sweeps a large area, striking incoming techniques to the side. It has an inherent serious disadvantage in that the straight arm can never move far away from the body and still retain its effectiveness. This means that powerful incoming attacks must be swept to the side in the few remaining inches before they strike home.

Never, under any circumstances, should a lower parry block be allowed to block a front kick square-on. This is guaranteed to cause serious bruising (if you're lucky!) or a fracture (if you're unlucky!).

Kyokushinkai lower parry is performed from hourglass stance. The left arm extends diagonally downwards while the palm of the right fist is brought close to the left ear (**159**). The right arm then wipes down across the left as the latter begins to withdraw to the hip. A strong pulley action takes place and the blocking arm extends fully as the withdrawing arm comes to rest palmupwards against the ribs (**160**). The blocking forearm

▲ 161

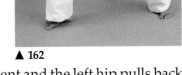

▲ 162

rotates through the movement and the left hip pulls back slightly to help the arm unroll.

Goju ryu block is performed in a similar manner except that, as we shall see, the blocking arm remains rather closer to the body. The sequence begins from an hourglass stance with the right arm brought down and across the body. The left is pulled back to the ribs. The right arm moves across the body as the left slides forward and overlays it. The right hand then withdraws powerfully to the ribs and the left cuts downwards and to the side of the body. Little forearm rotation is used.

Shito ryu lower parry begins from forward stance with the left arm extending forwards and downwards. The right is folded up and across the chest, with the palm turned back to the body (**161**). The left arm withdraws and rotates as the right cuts diagonally down and across the body (**162**). Strong forearm roation is used and body weight shifts behind the action to give added power.

▲ 163

▲ 164

▲ 165

▲ 166

The Shotokan sequence begins from right forward stance with the right arm extended downwards and the left on the hip. The back leg is brought forward and the left fist lifts across the chest, resting the little finger-edge down on top of the collar bone (163). The step continues on through and the blocking arm begins to curve downwards. As the step forward completes, so the left forearm rotates into its final position and the right pulls back to the hip (164).

The Wado ryu lower parry is only ever used in conjunction with a turn. The example begins from right reverse punch. The back foot slides across and the punching arm folds over the chest, so the little finger-edge of the fist is close to the body (165). The shoulders are then released and swing around behind the hips. The blocking arm thrusts downwards, twisting strongly into a palm-down configuration (166). The turning action provides most of the block's power requirement, with additional energy coming from the twisting motion of the forearm and a slight forward body movement.

The second and third blocks to be considered use a 'wiping' action of the forearm to clear attacks aimed at the face and body. These sweep quite a large area – the length of the forearm in fact – though this can be reduced by sloping the forearm away from the body. The blocking action is important insofar as the elbow and wrist should try to be in the same line. If the wrist or elbow lead, then the block is not everywhere simultaneous and in extreme cases, the attack can be inadvertently knocked down into the groin, or up into the neck and jaw.

Naming this block, even in English, poses problems

because what is 'inside forearm block' to one style is 'outside forearm block' to another. Therefore I will refer to them simply as 'forearm block #1' etc.

The Kyokushinkai version is performed from hourglass stance. The left arm fully extends and the right folds underneath it and across the body (167). The left arm is then withdrawn and the right moves away from the body, so they cross at the mid-way point. Movement is synchronised so the block completes as the left hand pulls in tightly against the ribs (168). Look again at the illustrations and note the rotation of the blocking forearm as it sweeps across the body. Although they are not visible, slight hip and shoulder actions provide additional power.

The Goju ryu version of forearm block #1 is characteristic of that style insofar as the blocking arm is held close to the body at all times, wiping over the chest and the other forearm. This, of course, reflects the closer engagement distance favored by this style. The technique begins from hourglass stance with the right blocking arm extended. The elbow bends 90 degrees and the top of the fist is level with the shoulder. The left fist pulls back to the side (169). The right arm folds closely across the chest and the left slides forward beneath it (170). The right arm is then drawn back as the left wipes up across the chest (171). There is a slight hip and shoulder involvement but no forearm rotation.

▲ 167

▲ 168

▲ 169

▲ 170

▲ 171

The Shito ryu block is performed from a forward stance. The right arm extends downwards and across the body as the left extends forward and above it (**172**). The left arm withdraws and the right sweeps up and across the body, the forearm rotating strongly as it goes (**173**). The action is short and crisp and is augmented by the left hip pulling back slightly. This helps the blocking arm to unroll outwards. A slight forward shift of the body's center of gravity helps 'set' the block.

Shotokan uses an extremely large movement which combines body momentum, the pulley principle and forearm rotation. It begins from a forward stance with an advancing step that brings the feet close together. The right hand extends directly forward with fingers ex-

tended and the palm turned downwards. The left wraps tightly across the body, the thumb-side of the fist pressing against the ribs. The step continues and the right hand is forcefully pulled back as the left moves away from the ribs (**174**). A new forward stance is adopted and the block completes. The right hand adds an extra flourish of power by clenching tightly into a fist and rotating strongly at the same time as the blocking arm (**175**).

The Wado ryu version is characteristic of that style in that no pulley action of any kind is used. Force for the block is developed from forearm rotation plus a combination of hip and shoulder action. The sequence begins from a reverse punch position with the right arm extended. This is followed by a step forwards during which

▲ 172

▲ 173

▲ 174

▲ 175

▲ 176

▲ 177

time the extended arm folds down across the body (**176**). The thumb-side of the fist touches the left ribs. The block then begins as weight settles on the new front foot. The forearm rotates until the thumb-side is facing outwards, the shoulders give a small shrug and the left hip pulls back imperceptibly to help unroll the block (**177**).

Forearm block #2 is an inherently more powerful technique since it makes better use of the strong chest muscles. It is a very punishing technique in the hands of a powerful exponent. Whereas forearm block #1 used the thumb-side of the forearm, so to speak, as the deflecting surface, this second block relies upon the little-finger-side of the forearm. The block wipes across the front of the body and must travel far enough for a complete

deflection. Many novices block only so far, leaving the attack to catch the chest a glancing blow.

One of the clearest demonstrations of how the basic block works can be seen from the Shotokan version. This begins from forward stance with the right arm extended down into a lower parry (**178**). During the step forward, the lower parry lifts and the fingers extend but the left fist remains against the side. As the step forward continues, so the extended right arm withdraws and the left lifts and bends, so the thumb-side of the fist comes near to the left ear (**179**). As the new stance settles, the left arm wipes across the body, pulled by the withdrawing right. The latter closes tightly into a fist just as the block completes (**180**). A strong forearm rotation is used.

▲ 178

▲ 179

▲ 180

▲ 181

▲ 182

▲ 183

▲ 184

▲ 185

▲ 186

▲ 187

▲ 188

The Shito ryu block is quite similar, though the extended hand is in the form of a fist. This is pulled back, so the right shoulder advances and the block swings across the front of the chest. Forearm rotation adds additional strength to the block.

The basic Kyokushinkai version begins from an hourglass stance with the blocking arm raised high and behind the head. The non-blocking arm that will provide the pulley action is folded across the upper chest, so the elbow points forward (181). The right arm is then withdrawn and with it comes the blocking forearm. Both shoulder and hip participate in this action. The right fist pulls back to the ribs and the blocking arm continues on until the attacking technique is swept clear of the body (182). Note the pronounced hip and shoulder position. Goju ryu uses a similar action but the arms are kept closer to the body. Hip and shoulder action combine to power the block.

Wado ryu is again the odd one out, using no pulley principle and relying instead upon a powerful hip action coupled with a forward shift in the body's center of gravity. Typically the sequence is performed on the move. In this case the opening technique is a reverse punch (183).

This swings wide of the body as the step forward progresses, turning the thumb-side of the fist in the direction of the head (184). A slight hip and shoulder movement then sweep the block back across the body, the forearm rotating as it goes (185).

Knife block uses a different action to cut incoming techniques to the side. The blocking agent here is the knife edge of the hand; that is to say, the little finger-edge. A pulley action takes place in all cases, with both hip and shoulder acting in support. The blocking forearm always rotates.

The first to be considered is the Shito ryu version. This begins from cat stance, with the leading arm inclining forward, palm to the front. The rear hand locates palm-upwards on the chest (186). The opening move of the step forward is accompanied by a strong hip and shoulder action, with the left hand curving over the top of the right and turning so the palm is directed towards the face (187). The step then takes place and the left hand cuts across in a blocking action as the right pulls back in front of the chest (188). The knife hand twists palm-forwards during the last few seconds of arc.

The Shotokan version is performed from a back stance.

▲ 189

▲ 190

The right hand extends palm-downwards as the back foot comes alongside the supporting leg. The left hand folds back over the shoulder, so the open palm is near to the ear. As the step progresses, so the right arm pulls back and the left slides down and across it (**189**). The blocking arm then cuts outwards, coming to a stop as the

new stance is set up (**190**). An often overlooked point is that the blocking action comes equally from the arm itself plus a twisting away of the shoulders.

The Wado ryu version is also performed from back stance but the leading arm is vertical and not inclined as it is in the two previous examples. This arm drops as the

▲ 191

▲ 192

▲ 193

▲ 194

step takes place and the original rear hand wraps around the upper chest (**191**). Note that the right palm is almost touching the left ear. The left arm then withdraws as the right cuts across the face (**192**). The left shoulder pulls back strongly to support the blocking action.

Goju ryu uses an interesting variation in which the palm tilts outwards. This imparts a drawing action to the block. The sequence begins from cat stance with the right arm slipping underneath the left elbow (**193**). The right arm does not change its position as the left comes in close to the body. Then the right arm is part withdrawn as the left begins sliding up and across the face of it (**194**). The block completes with the left hand tilting outwards. The right remains palm-forwards against the chest. All

action is therefore strictly contained within the outline of the body. The closer the elbow remains to the body, the stronger the block becomes.

Kyokushinkai uses a circular knife block to sweep a truly prodigious area clear of attacking techniques. It begins from a cat stance with both hands extended downwards above the leading knee. Both hands then move back together towards the rear hip (**195**) and circle upwards (**196**) before separating and dropping downwards into the final position (**197**). The initial part of the movement could be used against a kick, linking under the outstretched heel and drawing the opponent forward and off-balance. The gradual lift would then force him backwards.

▲ 195

▲ 196

▲ 197

The scooping blocks use circular actions to lift an incoming kick and draw it out. Typically the fingers are extended and therefore vulnerable to injury. It follows that a high skill level is necessary to use these blocks safely. The Shotokan version begins from ready stance with a step forward into back stance. The left hand extends and the fingers open; the right turns palm-upwards in front

▲ 198

▲ 199

▲ 200

▲ 201　　　　　　　　　▲ 202　　　　　　　　　▲ 203

▲ 204　　　　　　　　　▲ 205　　　　　　　　　▲ 206

of the belt (198). The blocking action is powered by the right hand withdrawing to the hip and thus drawing the left down in a scooping action (199).

The Wado ryu version is similar exept that it is powered by a substantial hip twist that turns the whole body sideways to the attack. Otherwise the scooping action is similar to that of Shotokan. Sometimes the turning action is accompanied by a slight sidestep to take the body out of line of the attack. There is also a reverse scooping action that turns the body in the opposite direction. One of the drawbacks with both of these blocks is that they limit the user's immediate counter-offensive capability. The hips must always return to forwards-facing before an effective punch can be used.

The Shito ryu version brings both shoulder and hip forward in an upwards travelling block (200) that knocks an attacking punch upwards. Note the face guard.

Goju ryu uses the back of the wrist in an upwards travelling block (201). Power is generated in the arm itself and there is neither hip nor shoulder involvement. Following this action, the palm of the hand is thrust strongly

down (202). Note the guard retained in front of the chest.

Double blocks sweep a great area of the head and body free of incoming attacks. The Goju ryu version keeps the arms close to the body and begins from an hourglass stance with the left arm extended downwards in a lower parry while the right is lifted as in forearm block. The right fist then moves downwards with a circular action, passing inside the similarly moving left (203). The crossing point occurs in front of the chest. From thence the left hand circles upwards as the right drops down (204). The final block has both deflecting forearms slightly to the outside of the body.

The Kyokushinkai version is very similar except that the arms are held further away from the body. There is little shoulder action, though the hips do move slightly from side to side. Wado ryu uses an almost identical sequence of moves but adds a definite whiplash hip movement to a fast arm movement. The Shito ryu version is demonstrated in an open handed version (205 & 206). Again, the arms move in fully circular paths, accompanied by a double hip twist.

SPARRING

◀ 207   ▲ 208   ▲ 209   ▲ 210

Funakoshi Gichin strongly opposed the introduction of free sparring into karate training, though he approved of prearranged practice. Free sparring allows an unprogrammed exchange of techniques though this is not to say that any technique can be used. For example, spear thrusts to the eyes and kicks to the knee joints are generally excluded. There is usually also a limitation to the amount of face contact permitted. Some systems allow full contact to the body; others permit powerful kicks to the head. Most permit reasonable contact to the body and only the lightest of face contact.

Prearranged sparring provides both partners with the knowledge of what attacking technique is to be used and in most cases, what response will be made to it. This does not prevent some quite elaborate sequences from being built up and in some cases, these appear indistinguishable from free sparring proper. Contemporary reports of prearranged sparring at Funakoshi's dojo indicate that it was taken very seriously indeed, with no quarter given or expected.

Every school of karate teaches prearranged sparring and this generally takes the form of a series of linear attacks, which the defender systematically counters as s/he steps back. There may be a five step sequence, a three step, or a one step sequence. The attack proceeds at a measured rate, giving time for each technique to be countered before proceeding. Both partners pause after the final exchange and withdraw into fighting stances to conclude the sequence.

In the following example from Shotokan, the attacker steps back with his right leg and blocks downwards into lower parry. The opponent stands in ready stance (**207**). The opponent steps back into forward stance and uses head block to deflect the attacker's head punch (**208**). With scarcely a pause, the attacker takes a second step and punches to mid-section. The opponent withdraws from this too and counters with forearm block #2 (**209**). Next the attacker uses a front kick but the opponent counters by stepping back and performing lower parry (**210**). The opponent then performs reverse punch even as the deflected foot is falling to the mat (**211**).

This is a fairly typical three step sequence but others are more complex. For example, the Wado ryu *Kihon* series uses quite complex evasions/counters. Both partners take up fighting stances and adjust the range

▲ 211

▲ 212

▲ 214

▲ 213

between them (**212**). The attacker slides forward on his front foot and punches to the opponent's head. The latter pulls back into a straddle stance, deflecting the punch with an elbow block (**213**). After only the briefest of pauses, the attacker then performs reverse punch. The opponent twists his hips to face the attacker, drawing back his leading foot as he does so. Simultaneously he blocks across the front of his face (**214**). The trick here is to evade by only the smallest distance so it is possible to slide along the outside of the punching arm and deliver a blow into the attacker's armpit.

Sometimes the attack consists of a single move but the response involves multiple techniques. Goju ryu exponents spar from closer range than other styles and here the attacker has thrown a punch at the opponent's midsection. This has been blocked with knife hand, followed by an immediate spear thrust to the eyes (**215**). Then the left blocking arm slides over and under the extended punching arm, locking the elbow straight. The right hand seizes the attacker's throat and is braced by the left (**216**). If this were not more than enough, the opponent then knees the attacker in the groin (**217**) and will finish by throwing her across his right thigh!

Looking at the matter logically, prearranged sparring provides a natural progression from basic techniques through to free sparring. It allows techniques to be tested in safety, yet with a measure of realism. But free sparring requires a high skill level if injuries are to be kept down. It follows then, that if a novice cannot pull back the toes during a front kick, then such a technique should not be used in free sparring. The same, of course, goes for any technique. Despite this rather obvious fact, many

▲ 215

▲ 216

▲ 217

schools have given in to their members and allow complete novices to free spar.

It used to be the case that at least one school banned free sparring until students reached brown belt grade. Unfortunately, student demands forced the abandonment of this admirable rule.

Competition karate is an extension of free sparring and all the styles described in this book practise it in one form or another. The most common form of competition is based upon a three point system which allows a limited accumulation of potentially effective techniques. The word 'potential' means that were the technique to be delivered with full force, the opponent would suffer serious injury. Furthermore, the technique must be performed in a technically correct manner – it is not enough to strike the opponent with any old punch or kick. It must be precisely ranged on the opponent because penalties are imposed for those which strike with too much force, or which strike a prohibited area.

The three point system succeeded the older one point system where a single mistake was enough to decide the outcome of a match. As you might imagine, this led to cautious engagements with limited spectator appeal. Shotokan schools still use the one point system though its usage has virtually ceased outside of that style.

Kyokushinkai has devised its own style of competition. This allows full-power kicks and punches to the body, and full power kicks to the head. The object is quite simple – knocking the opponent down with the force of a blow decides the outcome of a match. But despite the straightforward method of decision, the system still has drawbacks.

TRAINING METHODS

▲ 218

▶ 219

▲ 220

▲ 221

As I mentioned in the last chapter, karate is based upon a combination of the hard Southern Shaolin styles of kung fu with an Okinawan art that itself appears to be hard. The word 'hard' is used here in the technical sense of requiring obvious muscular power. Its opposite is 'soft', or 'internal', where the energy of impact is generated by less obvious means. It therefore follows that muscular exertion is required to produce the power inherent in karate techniques. How is this power to be generated?

Secondly, skill at karate techniques is obtained by constant repetition. This repetition must take place without fatigue, since that leads to a loss of efficiency in skill-learning. So how is the body trained to endure high-intensity workloads?

Thirdly, the leg techniques of modern karate require great hip flexibility. High kicks need sideways hip movement – or abduction as it is correctly called. The hamstring muscles must relax enough to allow the kicking foot easily to reach the opponent's face. And this flexibility must be available as the leg moves quickly – that is, dynamic flexibility. How is this flexibility arrived at?

Fourthly, the hands and feet must be tough enough to withstand high impacts on hard surfaces. How is this toughness generated?

Considering first the power requirement of karate, it is obvious that the faster a technique travels, the more energy it possesses. A technique travels quickly when the driving muscles – the 'agonists' – contract both strongly and quickly while the opposing muscles – the 'antagonists' relax. In other words, the correct group of muscles must be contracting and all others must not inhibit that action through their own tension. The second element is the mass of the weapon itself. There comes a time when speed of muscle contraction reaches its maximum for any individual. When that ceiling is reached, further gains in impact force can only be made by improvements in the strength of muscle contraction. Fortunately this is more open-ended.

It is certainly true that skill can make up serious deficiencies in power but ultimately it is worth reflecting that a good big 'un is likely to beat a good little 'un.

Traditional Chinese styles often made the would-be student perform menial tasks such as carrying water and doing chores. While this may well have been intended to make them value training when it eventually began, it might also have been intended as part of the physical preparation. Okinawan teachers sometimes did the same thing. Styles such as Goju ryu devoted a long period of initial training to preparing the body for the demands of practice. This training consisted of two elements, one in which the muscles of the body were pitted against each other and the other where weights were used.

When muscles work against each other, there is often no joint movement, even though the muscles are in a state of contraction. Try this out for yourselves. Interlock your fingers in front of your stomach and then try to pull your hands apart. If you grip hard with your fingers, then the triceps muscles on the back of your arms bulge but there is no movement at the joint. This is the principle used in low stances, where the leg muscles hold the limb bent against the force of gravity.

The kata *sanchin* pits one group of muscles against another so the whole body becomes rigid. This interferes with breathing, so breath escapes in short spasms. I should point out that all training of this kind raises blood

▲ 222

pressure because the muscles, when they contract, squeeze the veins and arteries they enclose and make it difficult to pump blood through them.

Though this kind of strength training does work, it produces strength known as 'isometric'. This is a fairly restricted kind of strength, since it is highly dependent upon the length of the muscle when it is being contracted. To get the maximum benefit from isometric training, you should vary the angle of the joints through which the muscles are acting.

Someone who follows this regime of training will make the body capable of withstanding severe blows. This is obviously an advantage, if it were not for several rather obvious drawbacks. The first is that the muscles cannot be kept constantly in a state of contraction – they must relax at some time or other. Any blow struck while they are relaxed may well cause injury. The second point is that it is difficult to move quickly when all your muscles are fighting against each other. The trick is to tense the muscles only when it is necessary to do so, relaxing immediately afterwards.

An alternative form of training uses external weights to load the body's muscles. Goju ryu use training weights consisting of a long barbell, two dumbbells, weighted sandals, the lollipop-like *chi'ishi*, stone filled jars and the iron ring, or *kongoken*. The barbell is used in a twisting action, rotating it vertically through 180 degrees. Sometimes it is rolled down the forearms to toughen them. The dumbbells are used to perform push-ups (**218**), or the feet can be hooked through them in a leg-raising exercise (**219**). Note that the leg is fully extended and the toes hook back to retain the dumbbell in position. Although the dumbbells are not very heavy, the fact that they are hanging on the end of a long limb increases leverage considerably.

The dumbbells are also used in a more orthodox manner. They can be lifted to the front, in the manner of a biceps curl (**220**), or lifted under the arms (**221**). They increase isometric loadings on the shoulders when suspended from the extended arms (**222**).

◀ 223 ▲224

▲ 225

▲ 226

▲ 227

▲ 228

Where there is joint movement against the weight, the exercise is said to be 'isotonic' and this is the method used chiefly in weight training gyms. If muscles are pumped quickly over a short time, then they increase both in the speed and strength of muscular contractions. If they are pumped over a long period, then they improve the ability to work without fatigue.

The iron sandals are also used in styles such as Wado ryu where they are held on by wrapping a karate belt around them and the instep of the foot. Straight leg lifts increase strength in the upper leg muscles. Bent leg lifts work the muscles involved in kicking.

The *chi'ishi* are mainstays of Goju ryu weight training practice. George Andrews makes them from cement into which he fits a wooden haft. The weight of the chi-ishi varies according to the size of the mold used and this alters the training effect. For example, a heavy chi'ishi moved slowly over a large number of repetitions builds local muscular endurance and slow-acting strength. A lighter chi'ishi moved quickly will produce a faster but weaker muscle contraction, with less of an endurance factor.

Training begin from a straddle stance, holding the chi'ishi at one end, so it dangles head down (**223**). The knees are straightened and the chi'ishi is swung around so the head is near the shoulderblade. Then it is drawn up and over the shoulder (**224**) before lowering it into an upright position with the arm at full extension (**225**). The body is lowered into a straddle stance once more as the arm is descending. Sometimes the forearm is twisted slowly, so the chi'ishi is lifted from head-downwards position. Each time, the stance raises slightly and then settles again as the final position is taken up.

Stone filled jars work the shoulders and forearms. The jars' neck size is critical insofar as it must allow the fingers to curl around it. At first the jars are used empty but as strength improves, more and more stones are added. The jars are placed within reach, then they are taken by their necks and lifted out and away from the body (**226**). The karateka steps from one hourglass stance to another, moving both forward and back. The training effect on the shoulders is varied by slightly changing the angle at which the arms are held.

Alternatively the jars can be lifted from a low straddle stance. The arms circle, so the jars pass to the front and to the rear in a coordinated swinging action (**227**).

The iron ring is another form of barbell used for isotonic/isometric strength and endurance work. It is lifted above the head as the karateka settles into a straddle stance (**228**). Alternatively, it is rested on the back of the neck during push-ups. This increases the loading on arm and chest muscles.

A training rig for developing exactly the right kind of strength required for punching has been devised by George Andrews. This takes the form of a wall-mounted pulley-weight system such that when a d-ring is pulled, a weight is drawn up. George stands with his back to the apparatus and grasps the d-ring in his closed fist. Then he punches slowly, so the weight is drawn up. By altering the weight lifted, he adjusts the intensity of work. The trick however, lies in the height of the d-ring. Most standard pulley systems operate at shoulder height. George's modified rig acts through the body's center of gravity, so power is applied when the fist is at stomach height. Correct application is essential, otherwise the upper body leans forward to get enough purchase.

Traditional martial arts used to use resisted/assisted work, harnessing the limb to be trained to a bamboo stem. The trainee then attempts to punch quickly against the bamboo's resilience. For spring assisted work, the bamboo cane is cocked by drawing the fist back to the hip. Then a punch is made so the bamboo adds a strong pull to the action. Care must be taken to ensure that the pull does not jerk the elbow straight, since this can lead to injury.

This principle of spring resisted/assisted work was revisited in the late 1960's when Kimura Shigeru of the Tani-ha Shito ryu began experimenting with motor car inner tubes. He anchored one end to the wallbars and grasped the other in his fist to punch against. Unfortunately there is one thing to beware of when using this system and that is, it invariably leads to unwelcome technique modifications. A punch does not offer increasing resistance to the muscles so when the trainee compensates for the stretching elastic, he unconsciously alters his stance and body angle in a way that is unsuitable for

▲ 229

▲ 230

the unloaded fist. The same drawback happens when you try to punch holding a dumbbell. The moving weight possesses considerable momentum which tends to keep moving forward even when the punch has ended. This leads to unwelcome stance changes.

Other schools of karate have also been deeply concerned with body preparation but rather than weights, they have relied upon body weight exercises. Push-ups are perfectly effective at increasing upper body strength and endurance.Explosive push-ups build fast, strong muscles. Many repetitions increase endurance in the shoulders and arm muscles. Push-ups with feet on a chair load the arms further. Some schools push-up on the knuckles. Others use the bowed fingers and, occasionally, only the thumb and another finger are used.

Sit-ups work the stomach muscles though they must always be practised with the knees bent. Straight leg sit-ups can cause back injuries because they tilt the pelvis to pull the upper body clear of the mat. Alter training effect by bending the knees to varying degrees. Bringing the heels close to the backside engages a different set of muscles to those used when the sit-up is made with nearly straight legs. Sitting-up with feet higher than head on an inclined surface increases the training effect; alternatively you can cuddle a weight to your chest to achieve the same result.

Squats work the thigh muscles used in kicking. However, never bend the knees more than 90 degrees since this can harm the knee joints. Some people add a high kick as they straighten from the squat position.

Strength building must always be accompanied by flexibility training. As muscles thicken and become strong, they also tend to shorten in length. This has the effect of limiting movement across a joint. Surprisingly, karate has paid little attention to those methods of joint stretching which safely approximate to the actual type of requirement. Normal static stretches – with the legs extended and the body inclining this way or that – do not

produce the mobility required during a kick. This may have been realised because one early exercise involved wearing the iron sandals mentioned above and swinging the legs hard to the front and sides. The momentum of the weight carried the limbs further than they would normally have gone.

We now know that this is extremely dangerous and far from improving flexibility, it is likely to reduce it! Better to build a platform of flexibility on the static pattern and then supplement it with dynamic mobility training consisting of high kicks – but without the weights!

My own theory is that high kicks were imported into karate without the accompanying exercise methods. If we look at the Korean analogue of karate – taekwondo – we see that an extensive repertoire of high kicks is accompanied by a relatively sophisticated selection of mobility exercises.

Endurance training varies according to what we are trying to achieve. A light training load can be sustained over long periods because the oxygen supply is sufficient to burn muscle fuel efficiently into carbon dioxide and water. Neither of these waste products creates a problem. When the pace of training steps up, however, oxygen demand outstrips supply and waste products such as lactic acid build up in the muscles, causing fatigue. The normal class lines of karate are excellent for improving aerobic endurance and kata are perfect for generating the right kind of anaerobic endurance. Some people spend time running long distances but ultimately, as the early teachers must have realised, that equips you to become marathon runners – not karateka. The trick is always to tailor your training to the skills you need to acquire.

The hands and feet must be toughened to withstand the effects of violent impact. Actually, the feet do not need much training since they are already calloused by the effects of walking. The knuckles, however, are different and require a program of toughening to make

▲ 231

▲ 232

▲ 233

them suitable for use as body weapons. The objects of this toughening process are to strengthen the bones of the knuckles so they can withstand damage and to increase the thickness of skin which covers them.

Traditionally, the knuckles were conditioned against a punching post known as a *makiwara*. The makiwara consists of eight feet or so of springy wood sunk three feet into the ground. The thickness of the post reduces towards the top, around which is bound rice straw. Modern training halls substitute smooth rubber since this is more hygienic. The karateka stands with the left foot leading and the right arm drawn back. The hips are turned 45 degrees away from the post. The hips twist square-on and after a slight delay, the punching arm follows. The fist does not rotate but is kept palm-downwards throughout. Impact is flush with the two major knuckles against the impact pad. The object is drive the post backwards with each blow. Provided this training is done frequently enough, the fist begins to form correctly – with impacts taking place only on the two largest knuckles.

The first few sessions bruise the knuckles and cause them to swell but this later abates and the bones increase in thickness to cope with the training load. Makiwara training should be followed by a massage of the knuckles using embrocation.

In Goju ryu the forearms too are toughened by the techniques of *kake*. These are clearly linked to the arm-toughening and awareness systems used by many Shaolin styles. Karateka stand close together with the backs of their forearms in contact (**229**). One pushes forward as the other yields, all the while maintaining a spring-like pressure (**230**). Then the roles change and the other pushes forward (**231**). The instant that pressure eases, the opponent rolls his hand free and attacks the other (**232**). Chi'ishi can also be used to toughen the forearms by rolling the haft along them while the weight bears downwards (**233**).

▲ 234

▲ 235

▲ 236

▲ 237

Kyokushinkai toughens the shins by using a padded pole braced by two students (234). Actually, the shin is an excellent body weapon and can be used against the opponent's head and upper leg.

Kimura Shigeru of the Tani-ha Shito ryu pioneered the use of the impact pad as a means of training to deliver high energy impacts on a moving opponent. This is a realistic training aid because the target has man-mass, so techniques are applied in exactly the right way. The impact pad consists of layers of closed-cell plastic foam welded together.

One person holds the pad against his chest, bracing it in such a way as to keep the fingers well clear of the impact area. The other stands at the correct distance and cocks his punch. The punch is delivered at full power, striking the pad square-on (235). Once this can be done accurately and safely, skill requirement is increased by moving the pad so the punch must compensate. Use the pad for straight kicks though take care because the legs are extremely powerful and generate a great deal of impact. Turning strikes can be put into the pad with full force, when the latter is turned sideways-on. This same orientation is used for turning kicks (236) but accuracy is of the essence. The versatile impact pad can also be held against the shin where it helps to perfect the footsweep (237).